HOW ANCIENT AMERICANS LIVED

JEN GREEN
MICHAEL STOTTER

southwater

This edition is published by Southwater

Southwater is an imprint of Anness Publishing Ltd
Hermes House, 88–89 Blackfriars Road, London SE1 8HA
tel. 020 7401 2077; fax 020 7633 9499
www.southwaterbooks.com; info@anness.com

© Anness Publishing Ltd 2005

UK agent: The Manning Partnership Ltd; tel. 01225 478444;
fax 01225 478440
UK distributor: Grantham Book Services Ltd; tel. 01476 541080;
fax 01476 541061
North American agent/distributor: National Book Network;
tel. 301 459 3366; fax 301 429 5746
Australian agent/distributor: Pan Macmillan Australia;
tel. 1300 135 113; fax 1300 135 103
New Zealand agent/distributor: David Bateman Ltd;
tel. (09) 415 7664; fax (09) 415 8892

Publisher: Joanna Lorenz
Editorial Director: Helen Sudell
Editor: Joy Wotton
Introduction: Jen Green
Designers: Sarah Williams, Caroline Reeves, Margaret Sadler
Illustration: Rob Ashby, Vanessa Card, Stuart Carter, Shane Marsh, Clive
Spong, Shane Watson
Photography: John Freeman
Stylists: Konica Shankar, Melanie Williams
Editorial Reader: Penelope Goodare
Production Controller: Claire Rae

A CIP catalogue record for this book is available from the British Library.

Previously published in two separate volumes as *Step Into the World of North
American Indians* and *Step Into the Arctic World*

Anness Publishing would like to thank the following children for
modelling for this book: Josie Ainscough, Laurence Ainscough, Jamal Ali,
Nathanael Arnott-Davies, Hazel Askew, Rhiannon Atkins, Harriet
Bartholomew, Sarah Bone, Trung Chu Vinh, Rory Clarke, Carissa Cork,
Louan Harrison, Stephanie Harvey, Daniel Haston, Kane Ives, John
Jlitakryan, Eka Karumidze, Muhammed Laher, Bianca Loucaides,
Monilola Majekodunmi, Salem Miah, Daniel A. Otalvora, Sarah Louise
Phillips, Ben Rodden, Carl Simpson, Simon Paul Anthony Thexton,
Shahema Uddowlla-Tafader, Isemfon Udoh.

PICTURE CREDITS
b=bottom, t=top, c=centre, l=left, r=right
AKG Photos 15r, 16l, 18l, 21br, 23tr, 25tc & bl, 26bl, 32bl, 33tr, 36b, 41l,
45t, 46bl, 47tl & b, 48bl & br, 54tl, 55tr, 60tr, 61t. Bryan & Cherry Alexander
66cl, 67c, cl & tl, 70c & tl, 71tl, cl & cr, 72bl & tl, 73tl, tr, cl & cr, 74 tl, bl
& br, 75cr, bl & br, 76 tl & cl, 77tr & cl, 78bl, 79c, 80tl, 81tl & tr, 82c & tl,
83cl & cr, 84cl & cr, 85tr & cl, 86c, 87tl & tr, 89ct & cr, 90cr, 91cl, 92tl, cl &
cr, 93tr, 94cl, 95cl, 97tl, 98tl, 100tl & bl, 101tr, cr, bl, & br, 103tl, 104tl,
105c & tl, 106c & tl, 107tl, cl & tr, 108tl, 109tr, cl & cr, 110cr, 111tl & tr,
112cl, 114tl & br, 115l & tr, 116bl, 117tl, tr & br, 118bl, 119tr, bl & br,
120tl & bl, 121 tr & br. The Art Archive 102tl. BBC Natural History Unit
/Jose Schell 83tr. Bridgeman Art Library 80cr, 99t, 102b, 103cl. Camera Press
112tl. Corbis 10, 11br, 16tr, 21tr, 23tl, 26br, 26c, 29tl & c, 32tr, 35c, 37tl
& br, 45br, 46tl, 48tr, 58tl, 59tl, c, bl & br, 62tl, 63tr, c, bc & bl, 79tl, 89cl,
91cr & tl, 98br, 99b, 104cr, 105cl, 111c, 114bl, 115cr. Corbis-Bettmann
17cl, 19tr, 20tr, 22tl, 24bl, 28c, 30b, 31bl, 33bl, 34bl, 37cl, 40br, 42bl, 44tl
& b, 45bl, 46br, 49t & cl, 51t, 53tr, 54bl, 55bl, 58b, 62bl & br. CM Dixon
11tl, tc & tr, 17tr & cr, 21bl, 23bl, 28l & tr, 29bl, 30tl, 35tr, 36tr, 37tr, 38l,
39tl, bl, c & tr, 40l, 41tr, 49bl, 50tl, 52tr, c & bl, 55tl & c, 56tl, 57tr, c &
bl, 61c. Mary Evans Picture Library 66tl, 85tl, 89tr, 90tl, 95tr, 103bl, 108cr.
Robert Harding /W. Herbert 93tl. Peter Newark's Pictures 14tl & tr, 15tl, 15tl
& tc, 17tl, 18tr, 20l, 21tl & tr, 23tc, 24tr, 25tr, 26tr, 27tl, 29bl & tr, 31c, 33tl,
34tr & br, 35tl & bl, 37bl, 38tr, 40tr, 42tr, 43tl & bl, 47tr, 49br, 50tr & b,
51b, 52bl, 56br, 60br. Oxford Scientific Films/Doug Allen 93tl, /R & J Kemp
86tl, 88tl, /M Penny 121tl. Planet Earth 91tr, 118tl, /B & C Alexander
78tl, /J Eastcott 83tl, 101tl, /F. Jack Jackson 88tl, 94tl, 95tl, /L Murray
115bl, /T Walker 96tl, 97tr. Scanpix Norge: 121cl. Scott Polar Research
Institute 110tl, 113tl, 116tl, 117cl. Tony Stone Images/J Balog 79tr, /PH
Cornutt 81cl, /Natalie Fobes 75tl, /Derke-O'Hara 87cl, /George Lepp 73br.
10 9 8 7 6 5 4 3 2 1

CONTENTS

Introduction

WHALE-HUNTERS AND WARRIORS

Five hundred years ago, the vast lands of the Americas were unknown to Europeans. Yet hundreds of different tribal groups were living there. Each had its own language, customs and way of life. Some groups lived as hunters, while others were farmers. Some had settled in one place, while others were wandering nomads. In each area, people had developed a lifestyle that was suited to the environment in which they lived.

WILD HORSES
Hunting over land was traditionally by foot. When horses were introduced to North America in the early 1500s, they transformed the lives of the Plains Indians. It meant they could expand their hunting area and made hunting much easier.

A FROZEN LAND
The Arctic is one of the harshest environments on Earth. Arctic peoples survived by hunting animals for meat, skins for clothes and shelter, and bones for tools and weapons.

THE FIRST AMERICANS

Human settlement of the Americas dates back at least 12,000 years. Some historians believe the first peoples arrived much earlier, as long as 40,000 years ago. These original settlers came from north-eastern Asia. They reached North America by way of a bridge of land that connected Siberia and Alaska during the last Ice Age, when sea levels were lower than they are today. Some of these early inhabitants remained in the far north. The ancestors of the Inuit and other groups spread slowly eastward as far as Greenland. Other tribes gradually moved south, some settling where conditions were favourable, and others moving on, so that all parts of the Americas were inhabited by around 10,000 years ago.

VARIED HABITATS

The North American continent spans a huge range of climates, from polar to tropical. By AD1500, people were living in every kind of habitat, from woodlands and prairies, to the mountains and swamps. In the far north and much of the southwest, the environment was hostile, with icy wastes and treeless moorlands in the north, and scorching deserts in the south. Yet even in these harsh places, people had learned the survival skills they needed not just to hang on to life, but to thrive.

WATER WAYS
Much of North America is covered with rivers, streams and lakes, and tribesmen became skilled boatbuilders, using *kayaks* and canoes to travel long distances.

WAYS OF LIFE

The very first Americans were
hunter-gatherers. They lived as
nomads, moving from place to
place as they hunted wild beasts,

fished in rivers, and gathered nuts, fruits and berries. Around 1000BC,
some groups became farmers. They cleared the land with simple tools,
sowed seeds and tended crops until it was time for harvest.

BOAT TRIP
Native Americans used canoes
to transport families across
stretches of water and ferry
heavy loads from place to place.

FARMING FOR FOOD

As farming developed, many groups were able to grow more food than they needed. The main crops
grown were maize, beans and squash, but tomatoes, asparagus and vanilla were also cultivated. The
surplus (extra) meant that some people were freed from farmwork, to make tools and other useful
items that could be traded for food or other goods. When the secret of making clay
pottery was discovered, some people became expert potters, while others became
skilled weavers, or leather- and metal-workers. As societies became more
organized, strong leaders emerged to take charge of each group.

In some parts of North America, fertile areas were permanently settled, and
the first villages grew up. Other areas were rich in game or less suitable for
farming. In the far north, the Inuit moved between traditional hunting grounds,
while the peoples of the Great Plains mainly lived by hunting buffalo. Most wars
between tribes were fought over land or hunting territory.

WARRIOR BRAVES
Each tribe had a war
chief who was in
charge of planning
attacks to expand their
hunting territory. As
the Europeans began to
occupy more land, many
tribes fought to stop them.

FOLLOWING THE HERD
Before the 1700s, there were massive herds of
bison. The Great Plains were virtually treeless
with vast areas of grass to feed the large animals.
The Plains covered an area of about 1,200km by
2,000km and hunters often had to travel for days
to glimpse a herd.

AT HOME

The first Americans lived in many different types of dwellings, depending on the climate and the natural materials available. Wood, stone, turf, animal hides, bones and mud bricks were all used to make dwellings of various sizes and shapes. Eastern groups such as the Iroquois and Secotans lived in wooden longhouses or domed wigwams. Plains Indians lived in cone-shaped tipis covered with buffalo hide. Arctic groups built stone and turf lodges with whalebone rafters, or igloos from snow blocks. The Pueblo peoples of the southwest constructed flat-roofed dwellings with sun-dried bricks.

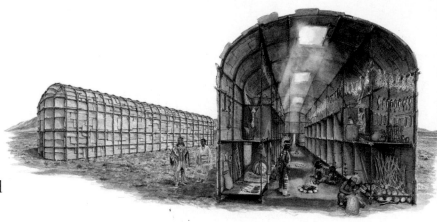

THE LONGHOUSE
Houses had to be adapted to their surroundings. In the east, where wood was plentiful, the Iroquois people built massive wooden houses, up to 45m long, with a barrel-shaped roof. Many families lived in each longhouse.

HOUSE OF BONES
The Inuit used whalebone rafters to support the roof of their homes. They would dig a pit to make the floor, build low walls and then use long bones for the roof.

FAMILY AND CLAN LIFE

Tribal groups varied in size from just a few families to large communities with over a thousand members. Each developed its own customs and religious beliefs, to explain where people had come from, why they lived as they did, and what happened when they died. Most groups believed the spirits of the ancestors lived on to influence the world of the living. People who were especially skilled at interpreting natural signs, or in the use of medicinal herbs, became respected as shamans (priests) or healers. Religious leaders conducted ceremonies to honour the spirits and celebrate the seasons.

Clan and family life were very important. Boys and girls were taught skills from an early age, but there was still plenty of time for fun and games, and for storytelling, singing, music-making and dancing. At regular times, many groups would meet with their neighbours for trading and celebrations, and sometimes sports such as racing, wrestling and archery.

REVEALING DREAMS
Woodland Indians painted symbolic pictures showing spirits worshipped by the tribe or dream images.

THE COMING OF THE EUROPEANS

Vikings were almost certainly the first Europeans to make contact with Native Americans. Around AD1000, these northern seafarers established several short-lived small colonies on the eastern shores of North America. In 1492, Italian sailor Christopher Columbus landed in the Bahamas, and later on the mainland. Other explorers quickly followed. Europeans had soon mapped the entire eastern coast of the Americas, which they called the "New World".

From the 1500s, increasing numbers of Europeans crossed the Atlantic. Spanish, French and English adventurers laid claim to lands where Native Americans had lived for centuries, and founded colonies (overseas territories) there. From the east coast, the colonists pushed westward, fighting wars with one another and with Native Americans to add to their territories.

SETTING SAIL
In 1492, Christopher Columbus set sail from Spain in the *Santa Maria* in search of a trade route to India. He never reached Asia, but landed first in the Bahamas and later on the mainland. He claimed the islands for the Spanish Empire.

TRADING WITH THE ENEMY
During the 1800s and early 1900s, European merchants made huge profits by buying otter, fox and mink fur, which had become incredibly popular in Europe. The merchants paid Arctic hunters low rates for trapping these valuable animals.

ANCIENT AMERICA TODAY

Native American arrows, spears and tomahawks were no match for the guns and superior technology of the Europeans. Quelling fierce resistance and breaking negotiated settlements, the colonists pushed on into the "Wild West". Many Native Americans were driven off their lands and forced to trek long distances to live on reservations.

The first Americans were rarely treated as equals. They were forced to give up their cultures for a way of life that suited the Europeans. However, their beliefs and customs did not die, but were handed down and survive today. Some groups have won compensation for their lost lands, while large homelands have been handed back to groups such as the Inuit, in the far north.

UNDER ATTACK
In 1864, 300 Cheyenne women and children were killed by US soldiers in the Sand Creek Massacre.

North American Indians

If you could travel back in time to AD1500,
you would find hundreds of different tribal
groups living in the woodlands, plains,
deserts, and icy wastes of North America.
Groups such as the Iroquois, Cherokee and
Secotans were skilled farmers, while the
Sioux and Blackfoot
tribes lived by hunting
the mighty buffalo
on the Great Plains.
Make your own tipi,
design a war
shield and build
a canoe that floats
as you explore
the world of
ancient America.

The First Americans

DESCENDANTS OF THE ANASAZIS, who were among the earliest known North American Indians, have colourful tales of their origins. One story tells how their ancestors climbed into the world through a hole. Another describes how all of the tribes were created from a fierce monster who was ripped apart by a brave coyote. The early history of the many nations or tribes is not clear, though archaeological finds have helped to build a picture of their way of life. If you could step back to before AD1500, you would find that the United States and Canada were home to hundreds of different Indian tribes. Each had its own leader(s) and a distinctive language and culture. Some tribes were nomadic, some settled permanently in large communities. Remains of pottery, woodcarvings and jewellery show how many of the North American peoples developed expert craft skills.

KEEPING THE PAST ALIVE
Descendants of the different tribes survive throughout North America, passing down stories and traditions to new generations. This boy in Wyoming is dressed in ceremonial costume for a modern powwow. He is helping to preserve his tribe's cultural history.

BRIDGING THE GAP
Archaeological evidence suggests that the first American Indians travelled from Asia. They crossed ice and land bridges formed at the Bering Strait around 13,000BC or earlier. From here, they moved south, some settling along the coasts.

TIMELINE 32,000BC–AD1400

Most historians believe that hunters walked to North America from Siberia. Evidence suggests there may have been two migrations – one around 32,000BC, the second between 28,000BC and 13,000BC. Some historians think there may have been earlier ancient populations already living there. More research is needed to support this theory. The hunters spread out, each group, or tribe, adapting their way of life to suit their environment. Later, some gave up the nomadic hunting life and began to settle as farmers.

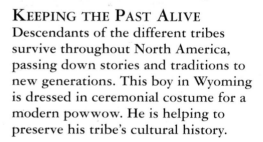

serpent mound of the Hopewell culture

3000BC Inuit of the Arctic are probably the last settlers to come from Asia.

1000BC Early cultures are mound builders such as the Adena and later, the Hopewell people. The Hopewell are named after the farmer on whose Ohio land their main site was found.

1000BC Farming cultures develop in the Southwest with agricultural skills brought in from Mexico.

black and yellow maize

300BC–AD1450 Cultures, such as the Hohokam, use shells as currency.

AD200 (or before) There is evidence of maize being grown by the mound-building people, probably introduced from Mexico.

AD700–900 Pueblo people bury their dead with black and white painted Mimbres pots.

burial pot

32,000BC

3000BC

300BC

BUCKSKIN RECORD

Tales of events were painted on animal skins, such as this one, created by an Apache. The skins serve as a form of history book. North American Indians had no real written alphabet, so much of the evidence about their way of life comes from pictures.

FALSE FACE

Dramatic, carved masks were worn by several tribes to ward off evil spirits thought to cause illnesses. This one is from the Iroquois people. It was known as a False Face mask because it shows an imaginary face. False Face ceremonies are still performed in North America today.

DIGGING UP EVIDENCE

Hopewell Indians made this bird from hammered copper. It dates back to around 300BC and was uncovered in a burial mound in Ohio. The mounds were full of intricate trinkets buried alongside the dead. Finds like this tell us about the crafts, materials and customs of the time.

ANCIENT TOWN

Acoma *(right)* is one of the oldest continuously inhabited traditional Pueblo settlements in the Southwest. It is still partly inhabited by Pueblo descendants. The Pueblo people were given their name by Spaniards who arrived in the area in 1540. *Pueblo* is a Spanish word meaning village. It was used to describe the kind of tribe that lived in a cluster of houses built from mud and stone. Flat-roofed homes were built in terraces, two or three storeys high.

AD700 Mound-building cultures build temples at Cahokia near the Mississippi. The city holds the largest population in North America before the 1800s.

AD900 Earliest Anasazis (ancient people) on the Colorado Plateau live in sunken pit homes. Later they build their homes above the ground but keep pit dwellings as kivas, which are their religious buildings.

AD982 First Europeans reach Greenland (north-east of Canada) under the Viking, Erik the Red.

AD1002 Leif Eriksson lands in Newfoundland, Canada, and creates the first European settlements.

Vikings arrive

AD1100 Anasazi people move into the mountains, building settlements in cliffs.

Mesa Verde, a cliff palace

AD1200 The Calusa in Florida are skillful carvers and craftsmen who trade extensively.

1270s–1300 Anasazis abandon many of their prehistoric sites and stone cities – many move eastwards.

1300 Beginnings of the Pueblo tribes (Hopi and Zuni) in the Southwest. Many of these are descendants of the Anasazis.

kiva (underground temple) of the Anasazis

Inhabiting a Vast Land

THE FIRST NORTH AMERICANS were hunters who followed musk oxen, bison and other animals to the grassland interior of the huge continent. Early settlements grew up in the rugged, hostile terrain of the Southwest where three dominant cultures evolved. The Mogollon (Mountain People) are thought to be the first Southwest dwellers to build houses, make pottery and grow their own food from around 300BC. The Hohokam (Vanished Ones) devised an extensive canal system to irrigate the desert as early as 100BC, while the Anasazi (Ancient Ones) were basket makers who built their homes high among the cliffs and canyons. In contrast, the eastern and midwestern lands abounded with plant and animal life. Here, tribes such as the Adena (1000BC to AD200) and the Hopewell (300BC to AD700), created huge earth mounds to bury their dead. The central Great Plains was home to over 30 different tribes, who lived by hunting bison. In the far north, the Inuit had a similar existence, relying on caribou and seals for their food and clothes. Europeans began to arrive around AD982 with the Vikings. Then in the 1500s, Spanish explorers came looking for gold, land and slaves. Over the next 400 years, many other foreign powers laid claim to different parts of the land. By 1910, the native population was at its lowest, about 400,000, and many tribes had been forced from their homelands on to reservations.

TRIBAL HOMELANDS

In the 1400s, there were more than 300 tribes, or nations, spread across North America (between two and three million people). These are often divided into ten cultural areas based on the local environment:
1 Arctic
2 Subarctic
3 Woodlands
4 Southeast
5 Great Plains
6 Southwest
7 Great Basin
8 Plateau
9 Northwest Coast
10 California.

TIMELINE AD1400–1780

Columbus

1400 Apaches arrive in the Southwest, probably by two routes – one from the Plains after following migrating buffalo, the other via the Rockies.

1492 Christopher Columbus sails from Spain to the Bahamas where he meets the peaceful, farming Arawaks.

1510 The powerful Calusas of Florida abandon their ancient centre, Key Marco, an island made from shells, possibly after hearing of foreign invaders.

1513 Calusas drive off Ponce de León.

1541 Zuni people get a first glimpse of horses when Spain's Francisco Vasquez de Coronado travels to the Southwest.

1541 Caddo people of the Plains oppose Spanish Hernando de Soto's soldiers.

1542 The large Arawak population that Columbus first encountered has been reduced to just 200 people. Ten years later the Arawaks die out through mistreatment.

shell wampum belt celebrates the League of Five Nations

1550 League of Five Nations is formed by the Seneca, Cayuga, Mohawk, Oneida and Onondaga tribes in the northeast to create a strong government. They are referred to as the Iroquois.

1585 Sir Walter Raleigh reaches the northeast coast and, ignoring the rights of the Secotan natives, claims the land for the English, calling it Virginia.

1590 Raleigh and John White return to Virginia, but the colony has disappeared. White draws pictures documenting Secotan life.

1400   1540   1550   1595

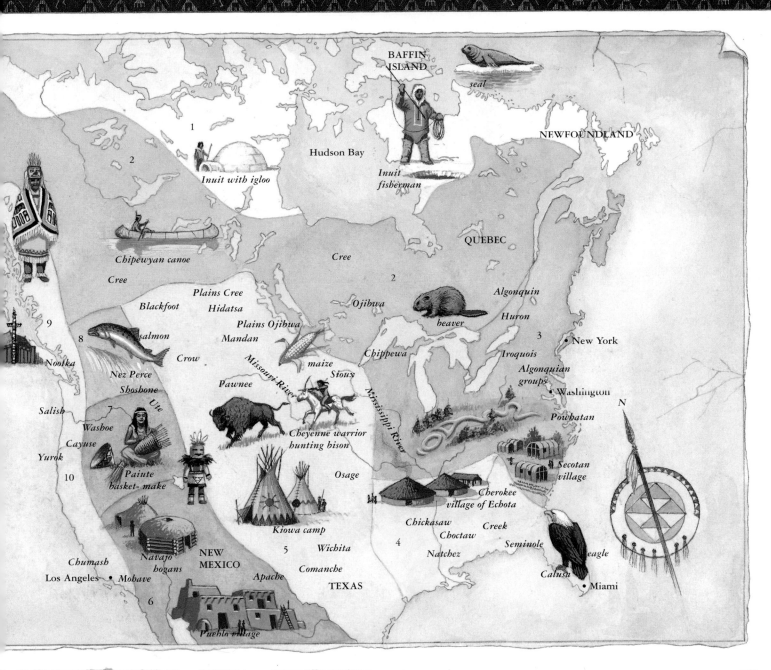

BAFFIN ISLAND

seal

NEWFOUNDLAND

1

2

Hudson Bay

Inuit with igloo

Inuit fisherman

QUEBEC

Chipewyan canoe

Cree

Cree

2

Plains Cree

Blackfoot

Hidatsa

Plains Ojibwa

Ojibwa

Algonquin

Huron

beaver

Mandan

9

8

salmon

Crow

Nez Perce

Shoshone

maize

Missouri River

Pawnee

Sioux

Chippewa

Mississippi River

Iroquois

New York

Algonquian groups

Washington

Nootka

Ute

Salish

7

Washoe

Cayuse

Yurok

Paiute basket-make

10

Cheyenne warrior hunting bison

N

Powhatan

Secotan village

Osage

Cherokee village of Echota

Kiowa camp

Chickasaw

Choctaw

Creek

Natchez

Seminole

eagle

Chumash

Navajo hogans

NEW MEXICO

5

Wichita

Comanche

TEXAS

4

Calusa

Miami

Los Angeles

Mohave

Apache

6

Pueblo village

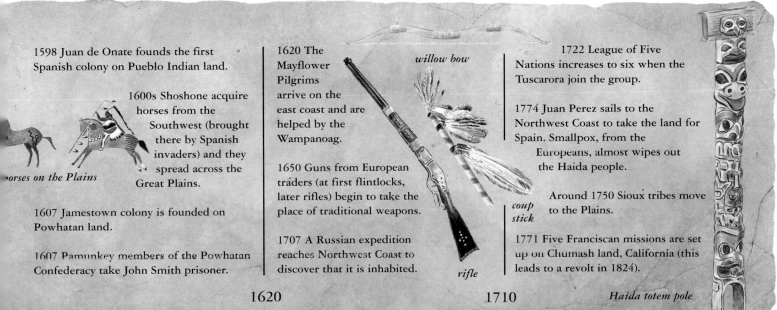

1598 Juan de Onate founds the first Spanish colony on Pueblo Indian land.

1600s Shoshone acquire horses from the Southwest (brought there by Spanish invaders) and they spread across the Great Plains.

horses on the Plains

1607 Jamestown colony is founded on Powhatan land.

1607 Pamunkey members of the Powhatan Confederacy take John Smith prisoner.

1620 The Mayflower Pilgrims arrive on the east coast and are helped by the Wampanoag.

willow bow

1650 Guns from European traders (at first flintlocks, later rifles) begin to take the place of traditional weapons.

1707 A Russian expedition reaches Northwest Coast to discover that it is inhabited.

rifle

coup stick

1722 League of Five Nations increases to six when the Tuscarora join the group.

1774 Juan Perez sails to the Northwest Coast to take the land for Spain. Smallpox, from the Europeans, almost wipes out the Haida people.

Around 1750 Sioux tribes move to the Plains.

1771 Five Franciscan missions are set up on Chumash land, California (this leads to a revolt in 1824).

1620

1710

Haida totem pole

13

Brave and Bold

MANY NORTH AMERICAN Indians who have earned a place in history lived around the time that Europeans reached North America. They became famous for their dealings with explorers and with the white settlers who were trying to reorganize the lives of Indian nations. Some tribes welcomed the new settlers. Others tried to negotiate peacefully for rights to their own land. Those who led their people in battles, against the settlers, became the most legendary. One of these was Geronimo, who led the last defiant group of Chiricahua Apaches in their fight to preserve the tribe's homeland and culture.

POCAHONTAS (1595–1617)
The princess became a legend, and the topic of a Disney film, for protecting English Captain John Smith against her father, Chief Powhatan. The English took Pocahontas captive to force Powhatan's people to agree to their demands. She married John Rolfe, an English soldier, and in 1616 left for England with their baby. She never returned, as she died of smallpox, in Gravesend, Kent, aged 22.

CORNPLANTER (died 1796)
In the 1700s, Cornplanter was a chief of the Iroquois Confederacy. He was a friend to the Americans and fought on their side in the Revolution of 1776–85. Seneca lands were spoiled but Cornplanter's people were given a reservation for their help. Many Iroquois people fought on the side of the British which split the group.

Opechancanough, Powhatan

Black Hawk, Sauk

Geronimo, Apache

Pontiac, Ottawa

Lapowinsa, Lenape

TIMELINE AD 1780–1924

1783 The colonists (settlers) sign a treaty with Britian which recognizes their independence and calls them Americans. The tribes are never regarded as American.

1788 The Chinook in the Northwest have their first encounter with Europeans when they meet Englishman, John Mears.

1789 Explorers encounter Kutchin and other Subarctic tribes, who later set up trade with the Hudson's Bay Company (formed in 1831).

1795 Tecumseh refuses to sign the Treaty of Greenville giving up Shawnee land.

William Clark and Meriwether Lewis

1803 The US federal government buys Mississippi land from the French, squeezing out the Indians even more.

1804 Sacawagea guides Lewis and Clark on the first overland journey from Mississippi to the Pacific Coast.

1830–40s Painters such as Frederic Remington, George Catlin and Karl Bodmer, document lifestyles of the Plains Indians.

1832 Sauk chief, Black Hawk, leads a final revolt against the US and is defeated.

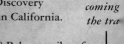
coming the tra

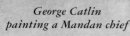
George Catlin painting a Mandan chief

1848 Discovery of gold in California.

1848–58 Palouse tribe of the Plateau resist white domination, refusing to join a reservation.

1780

1803

1848

SARAH WINNEMUCCA (1844–1891)

Sarah was from the Paviotso Paiutes of northern Nevada. Her grandfather escorted British Captain John Fremont in his exploration of the West in the 1840s. But in 1860 her mother, sister and brother were all killed in the Paiute War against white settlers. Sarah acted as a mediator between her people and the settlers to help improve conditions. She later wrote a book, *Life Among the Paiutes,* telling of the suffering of the tribe and her own life.

TECUMSEH (died 1813)

A great chief of the Shawnees, Tecumseh, tried to unite tribes of the Mississippi valley, Old Northwest and South against the United States. He even fought for the British against the US in the 1812–14 war. The picture shows his death.

SITTING BULL (1831–1890)

The Hunkpapa Sioux had a spiritual leader, a medicine man known as Sitting Bull. He brought together sub-tribes of the Sioux and refused to sign treaties giving up the sacred Black Hills in South Dakota. He helped to defeat of General Custer at Little Bighorn.

Oscelo, Seminole

Red Cloud, Sioux

Chief Joseph

PROTECTING THEIR TRIBES

These eight North American chiefs are some of the most famous. Not all fought. Lapowinsa of Delaware, was cheated out of land when he signed a contract allowing settlers as much land as they could cover in a day and a half. Pontiac traded with the French but despised English intrusion. Chief Joseph tried to negotiate peacefully for land for the Nez Perce tribe but died in exile. Red Cloud successfully fought to stop gold seekers invading Sioux hunting grounds.

1850s–80s Railways open up the West to settlers.

1850 The Navajo sign their third treaty with the US but hostilities continue.

1864 The Long Walk – Navajo people and animals are massacred by US troops, their homes burned. Survivors are forced to walk 500km to Fort Sumner.

1864 Sand Creek Massacre – 300 Cheyenne women and children are killed by US soldiers.

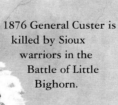

Sand Creek Massacre

1876 General Custer is killed by Sioux warriors in the Battle of Little Bighorn.

1886 Surrender of Geronimo to the US. He is a prisoner for many years.

1890 Ghost dance springs up as Sioux tribes mourn their dead – it worries the white settlers who see it as provocation.

1890 Sitting Bull is killed at Standing Rock (a Sioux reservation) by Indian police hired by the US.

1890 Sioux chief Big Foot and many of his tribe are killed in the Massacre of Wounded Knee. This ends the Sioux's struggle for their homelands.

1924 US citizenship granted to American Indians and marked by a coin bearing a buffalo.

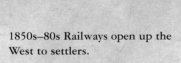

Buffalo coin

Ghost dance shirt

1870

1924

Nomadic Life

MANY TRIBES, such as the Cheyenne and Arapaho of the Great Plains, were nomadic. Their life was regulated by the bison who supplied them with their food, clothing and shelter. There were also semi-nomadic tribes such as the Pawnee, who spent part of their time in permanent lodges but sometimes wandered on to the Plains to hunt bison. Others, like the Inuit in the Arctic and the Pima of the Southwest, lived in villages but moved with the changing seasons. American Indians believed that the land was a source of life, filled with spirits. They lived in harmony with nature, adapting themselves to their surroundings. In contrast, the white settlers believed that they owned the land, and built

permanent towns that changed the landscape.

FOLLOWING THE HERD
A hunter on horseback catches up with two bison. Before the 1700s, there were massive herds of bison. The Great Plains were virtually treeless with vast areas of grass to feed the large animals. The Plains covered an area of about 1,200km by 2,000km and hunters often had to travel for days to glimpse a herd.

FREE LIVING ON THE PLAINS
Groups of women and children moving home across the Great Plains were a common sight. The men would often travel behind the convoy to guard the families from surprise attacks. A travois (carrying frame) was one of the most effective ways of carrying tipis and clothes. It was simply two long poles fixed together. Bundles of possessions were strapped in the centre, and sometimes children sat on it.

MAKE A TIPI

You will need: an old double sheet (or fabric measuring approx 250cm x 78cm), scissors, pencil, ruler/tape measure, large and small paintbrushes, yellow, blue and red acrylic paints, water pot, 12 bamboo sticks 3m long, rope or string, three small sticks, large stones (optional).

1 Lay the sheet flat. In the centre of one longer edge, cut a semicircle 46cm across and 20cm deep. Cut the fabric into a semicircle 152cm deep all round.

2 Measure, then make, three evenly spaced small holes on each of the straight edges. Start 6cm in from the centre and 3cm in from the flat edge.

3 Using a pencil and ruler, draw out a geometrical pattern of triangles, lines and circles. Make it bold and simple. Paint it then leave to dry.

CAMPING ON THE SHORES OF LAKE HURON

A group of Ojibwas go about their everyday business in a camp by Lake Huron. A woman is pounding corn in preparation for making corn mush. The men are resting by their birchbark canoes after a fishing trip. Their simple home is a conical form of the birchbark wigwam. Families would always try to pitch their homes near water.

WHALE KNIFE

This knife has a bone spear tip and shell blades. It was used by the Makah and Nootka whale hunters of the Northwest Coast who used it to cut away blubber.

TREASURED MEMORIES

An Arctic Inuit carved pictures on a walrus's tusk to record a great day's hunting caribou. Colour was added by rubbing a mixture of charcoal and grease into the etched lines.

MOVING ON

This family of Blackfoot Indians are migrating to Canada. They have few possessions. The homes of the nomadic tribes were easy to construct and easy to pack away when it was time to move on.

Your tipi is a simplified version of the Plains tipis. These were large, heavy constructions made of buffalo skin. They had a built-in smoke flap and a cut-out hole for the door.

4 Take three of the bamboo sticks and join them together at the top. Arrange them on the ground to form a tripod. Tie them securely.

5 One by one, lean the rest of the bamboo sticks against and around the tripod. Remember to leave a gap which will be your tipi entrance.

6 Now take the painted sheet (your tipi cover) and wrap it around the frame. Overlap the two sides at the top of the frame so that the holes join up.

7 Insert a small stick through the two top holes to join them. Do this for each of the other holes. Place stones around the bottom to secure your tipi.

Travel and Transport

NORTH AMERICAN INDIANS were often on the move, although walking was at first their only form of land transport. Hunting and trade were the main reasons for travelling. Young infants were carried in cradleboards, while Inuit babies were put into the hoods of their mothers' parkas. Travois were popular among those living on the Plains. These were frames dragged by dogs and later, horses. One strong dog could pull a load of 23kg. In the late 1600s, the Spanish introduced the horse, which the Crees called big dogs. This transformed Plains life, as tribes could travel greater distances to fresh hunting grounds.

WATER WAYS
A Kutenai Indian uses his birchbark canoe to paddle out to a clump of rushes. Much of North America is covered with rivers, streams and lakes, and tribesmen were skilled boatbuilders. There were kayaks (Arctic), bark canoes (Woodlands), and large cedar canoes (Northwest Coast).

ANCIENT TRACKS
Travelling over land was traditionally by foot. Indians made carrying pouches from animal skins which were tied to their backs by leather strips. For thousands of years, ancient trade routes connected villages that were hundreds of kilometres apart. Paths and trails were mainly formed by animals, either migrating or looking for food and water. Hunters found and used these trails which were often no bigger than the width of one person.

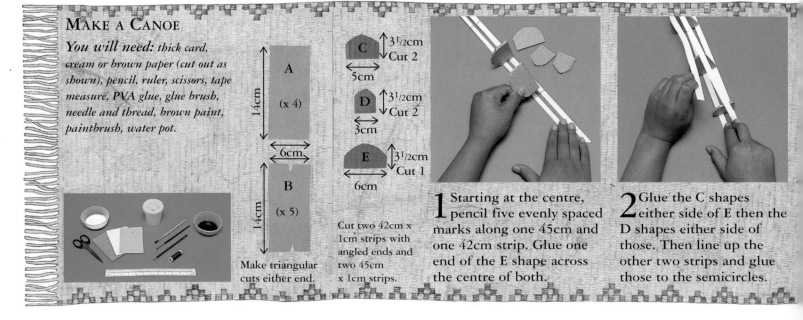

MAKE A CANOE
You will need: thick card, cream or brown paper (cut out as shown), pencil, ruler, scissors, tape measure, PVA glue, glue brush, needle and thread, brown paint, paintbrush, water pot.

A (x 4) — 14cm, 6cm

B (x 5) — 14cm

Make triangular cuts either end.

C — 3½cm, Cut 2, 5cm

D — 3½cm, Cut 2, 3cm

E — 3½cm, Cut 1, 6cm

Cut two 42cm x 1cm strips with angled ends and two 45cm x 1cm strips.

1 Starting at the centre, pencil five evenly spaced marks along one 45cm and one 42cm strip. Glue one end of the E shape across the centre of both.

2 Glue the C shapes either side of E then the D shapes either side of those. Then line up the other two strips and glue those to the semicircles.

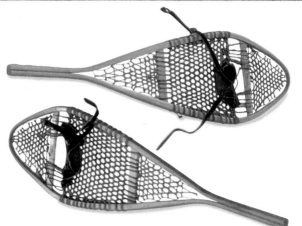

KEEPING YOUR BALANCE

In the north, walking on snow was aided by snowshoes so that even in deep snow a hunter could pursue his prey. Inuit, in the Subarctic and Arctic, used test sticks, similar to ski poles, to test the strength of ice.

TRAVOIS TRAVEL

Chief Eagle Calf is getting ready for a trip. The long poles of the travois are made into a V–shape and attached to the horse's saddle by leather thongs. The open ends drag on the ground. A carrying platform made of animal skin is stretched across the middle and lashed to the frame. This could be piled high with goods or children. It took two horses to carry the poles and covers of a single tipi.

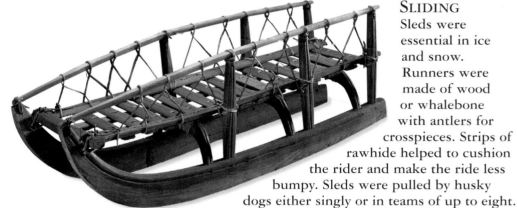

SLIDING

Sleds were essential in ice and snow. Runners were made of wood or whalebone with antlers for crosspieces. Strips of rawhide helped to cushion the rider and make the ride less bumpy. Sleds were pulled by husky dogs either singly or in teams of up to eight.

COLD HOMECOMING

In the snowy Arctic, Inuit used dogs to pull sleds. Dogs were no use over ice floes, so the Inuit pulled his own sled.

Birchbark canoes were made by the Chipewyan tribe in the Subarctic. They were used for crossing lakes and streams but also for fishing, farming and gathering rushes and wild rice.

3 Glue the two 45cm strips together then the two 42cm strips, at both ends. Glue shapes B to the frame, making sure the triangular cuts fit over C D and E.

4 Neaten the ends by gluing the excess paper around the frame. Place the A shapes over the gaps then glue to the top of the frame.

5 Continue sticking the rectangles of paper over, until all of the boat is covered. Now, carefully fold over and glue the tops of the paper all round.

6 Thread the needle. Using an overlapping stitch, sew all round the top edge of the boat to secure the flaps. Now you can paint your boat.

Tribal Society

A SINGLE TRIBE COULD BE AS SMALL as ten families or stretch to thousands. Neighbouring tribes would come together in times of war, for ceremonies and for trading, or to form powerful confederacies (unions). Some Algonquin people formed the Powhatan Confederacy, named after their leader, and controlled the coastal region of present-day Virginia. Other northeastern groups formed the League of the Iroquois to prevent conflict between local tribes. In the Southeast, the Creek, Seminole, Cherokee, Choctaw and Chickasaw were known by Europeans as the Five Civilized Tribes because of their system of law courts and land rights developed from European influences.

MAGNIFICENTLY COSTUMED
American Horse of the Oglala Sioux wears a double-trail war bonnet. His painted shirt shows he was a member of the Ogle Tanka'un or Shirt Wearers, who were wise and brave.

COMMITTEE MEETING
A Sioux council gathers to hear the head chief speak. Councils were made up of several leaders or chiefs. They elected the head chief whose authority came from his knowledge of tribal lore and skill as a warrior.

MAKE A HEADDRESS

You will need: ruler, 1m x 1cm red ribbon, red upholstery tape (75cm x 6cm), masking tape, needle, cotton, scissors, white paper, black paint, paintbrushes, water pot, 3mm diameter balsa dowel, PVA glue, 6 feathers (optional), white, red, yellow, light and dark blue felt, beads (optional), red paper, 20cm x 2cm lengths of coloured ribbon.

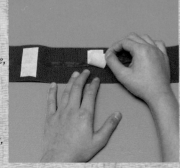

1 Lay the 1m length of red ribbon along the middle of the upholstery tape. Leave 12.5cm lengths at each end. Tape it in place while you sew it on.

2 Next make the feathers. Cut 26 feathers from the white paper. They need to be 18cm long and 4cm at their widest point. Paint the tips black.

3 When the black paint is dry, use the scissors to make tiny cuts around the edges of the paper feathers. This will make the paper look more like feathers.

WOMEN IN SOCIETY

The Iroquois women attended council meetings, but in most tribes women did not join councils or become warriors. Women held a respected place in society. In many tribes, such as the Algonquian, people traced their descent through their mother. When a man married, he left his home to live with his wife's family.

DISPLAYS OF WEALTH

Potlatch ceremonies could last for several days. The gathering was a lavish feast celebrated by tribes on the Northwest Coast. Gifts would be exchanged and the status of a tribe judged by their value.

IN COMMAND

This chief comes from the Kainah group of Blackfoot Indians. The Kainah were also known by Europeans as the Blood Indians because of the red face paint they wore. The Blackfoot headdress had feathers that stood upright as opposed to the Sioux bonnet which sloped backwards sometimes, with trailing eagle feathers.

FEATHER PIPE OF PEACE

North American Indians had a long tradition of smoking pipes. Plants were often smoked for religious and ritual reasons. Early peace talks involved passing around a pipe for all to smoke to show they had good intentions of keeping agreements.

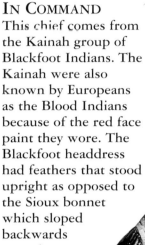

4 Cut the balsa dowel into 26 lengths of 14cm long. Carefully glue a stick to the centre of the back of each feather, starting just below the black tips.

5 If you are also using real bird feathers, tie them with cotton on to the bottom of six of the paper feathers. These will be at the front of the headdress.

6 Glue and tape the feathers on to the front of the red band, overlapping the feathers slightly. Position them so that the six real feathers are in the centre.

7 Cut 1cm x 6cm lengths of white felt. Glue them over each of the sticks.

Instructions for the headdress continue on the next page...

21

Dress and Identity

ONE OF THE MOST POPULAR images of a North American Indian is that of a warrior dressed in fringed buckskin with a war bonnet and decorated with body paint and beads. That was just one style of dress mainly used by the Plains Indians. Each nation, or tribe, had its own identity and distinctive clothing. Hunters dressed in animal skins and furs. In areas where agriculture dominated, cloth was woven from wild plant fibre or cultivated cotton. Tribes, such as the Navajo, began to use wool when the Spanish introduced sheep in the 1600s. Climate also dictated what was worn. In the cold north, the Inuit wore mittens, boots and hooded coats called parkas. These were made of seal or caribou skins with the fur worn on the inside. Many east coast and Woodlands men wore just loin cloths or leggings, while women wore fringed skirts.

HOPI GIRL
The squash-blossom hairstyle of this Hopi girl tells us that she is single. It was a symbol of maturity and readiness for marriage. Married women wore their hair loose or in braids. Hopi men wove cotton for blankets and clothes. The women would dye them.

NATURAL COLOURS
North American Indians made natural dyes and stains from the plants around them. Vivid reds, yellows, blues and greens could be produced by squeezing and grinding berries and nuts. Leaves and bark were also used.

blackberries

walnuts

raspberries

8 Cut out 1.5cm x 1cm pieces of red felt. Cut 3 for 10 of the feathers (5 each end) and 2 for the rest. Glue on to the white felt to make stripes.

9 Cut out a 40cm x 4cm yellow felt band. Decorate it by gluing on triangles of light and dark blue felt, and small squares of red felt.

10 You can also decorate it with beads. Carefully glue these on to the centrepiece, in the middle of the felt squares and triangles.

11 Very carefully glue the centrepiece on to the red band, using a ruler to help you place it in the middle. Some feathers will show on either side.

VERSATILE HAT
This early, woven spruce-root hat was worn by the Nootka on the Northwest Coast. It could also be used for carrying, storage or even as a fish trap. To make it, bundles of fibre were woven together then coiled into a spiral shape.

WORN WITH PRIDE
Scalplocks of human hair hang down the front of this hide shirt. These show that the Plains warrior who owned it had surpassed himself in battle. He would wear it with pride on ceremonial occasions. The shirt has been made from two deerskins stitched together.

TRADITIONAL CRAFTS
This woman wears a modern version of a cape. Woodlands and Plains people particularly liked the red and blue cloth brought by European traders.

BEADED WAISTCOAT
To decorate this man's vest the Sioux would have traded goods for glass beads brought to North America from Italy. Beads were traded by weight or by length, in strings. Before beads, the Sioux used porcupine quills to decorate their ceremonial dress.

Plains warriors had to earn the right to wear a headdress like this. Such a long and elaborate war bonnet would not usually be worn into battle, but kept for ceremonial occasions.

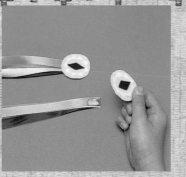

12 Draw a circle 3cm in diameter on the red paper. Then draw a 15cm tail starting at the circle. It should measure 1cm across and taper to a point.

13 Draw eight of these and cut them out. Glue them on to the ends of the feathers on the middle of the band so that the points stick into the air.

14 Cut out two circles of yellow felt, 5cm in diameter, and decorate with red and white felt shapes. Glue the coloured ribbons to the back of the circles.

15 Finally, glue or stitch the felt circles on to the headdress on top of the decorative band. The ribbons should hang down either side by your ears.

23

Ornament and Decoration

JEWELLERY, BODY PAINT and tattoos were worn by both men and women. Haida women tattooed their faces, bodies and the back of their hands with family symbols. The people of the Yuma wore minimal clothing so that they could display their tattoos with pride. Tattoos were simple, or elaborate such as the designs that decorated Timucua adults. These were coloured black, red and blue. A tattoo revealed status or was worn to gain protection from a spirit. A less permanent and painful form of skin decoration was created with face and body paints. Hairstyles also carried meanings. A particular style could indicate that a young man was unmarried, belonged to a military society or was a brave warrior. Woodlands men had a distinctive hairstyle. They braided their hair at the front and decorated it with turkey feathers. Some Plains warriors, such as the Pawnee and Iowa, shaved their heads completely, leaving a long tuft on top.

WAR PAINT
Mato-Tope, the chief of the Mandan people, put on his war paint just to have his picture painted. He was posing for the artist Karl Bodmer in 1834. Body paint was used to indicate a social position, and was usually applied for ceremonies and before going to war.

CHILDREN'S COSTUMES
These children were photographed in 1913. Even without being told the date, their costume gives away the era and the tribe they are from. This style of clothes was worn by the Sioux. The girl's hair is plaited with a centre parting. This was known as the reservation style because it was popular after the tribe had been moved on to official camps. Children's dress was usually a smaller version of adults' clothing.

MAKE A NECKLACE
You will need: white paper, ruler, PVA glue, brush for the glue, paints in blue, turquoise and red, paintbrush, water pot, scissors, air-drying modelling clay, barbecue stick/skewer, string.

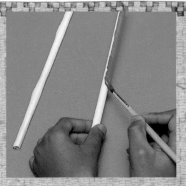

1 Roll up strips of thin white paper into 0.5cm tubes. Glue down the outer edge to seal the tube and leave to dry. Make three of these paper tubes.

2 Paint the rolls of paper. Paint one roll blue, one turquoise and one red, making sure that you cover all the white. Leave them to dry.

3 When dried, the painted paper tubes will have hardened slightly. Carefully cut the tubes into 1cm pieces to make little beads.

THE NATURAL LOOK

Body paints were extracted from raw materials. Red came from the earth with iron in it, and copper ore was used for green and blue. Charcoal gave a crisp black. Berries were used to stain faces and clothes.

charcoal

ochre

blueberries

MEDICINE MAN

This medicine man from New Mexico is wearing a head wrap. His beads, scarf and particularly the blanket wrap were popular among the Diné (Navajos). Other tribes wore head wraps, such as the Osage, who wore an otter-skin turban.

TATTOOED WOMAN

A Florida woman's body is covered with simple black band tattoos. They were etched by pricking the skin with needles dipped in vegetable dyes, and were worn by men and women.

DECORATIVE TEETH

An Inuit has carved ivory ornaments to make this necklace. Ivory comes from the tusks (canine teeth) of the walrus or the sperm whale.
Inuit use ivory as well as wood, bone, fur and feathers for jewellery, ceremonial masks and trinkets.

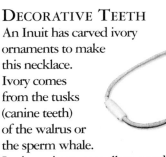

Indian craftmakers traditionally made beads like these from bone, stone and shell. Some of their bone beads were 8–10cm long. It was the European traders who brought glass beads over in the 1500s.

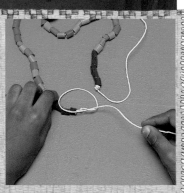

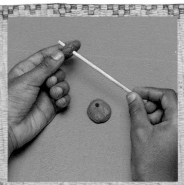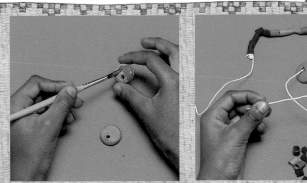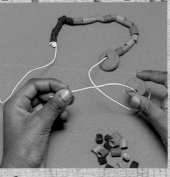

4 Make two larger clay beads by rolling the clay on a flat surface. When you are happy with their shape, pierce the centre with the stick.

5 Leave the clay beads to dry and harden. When they are ready, paint both of the beads blue (or your preferred colour). Once again, leave them to dry.

6 Thread the beads on to the string. Start with the clay beads which will hang in the centre. Then add the blue either side, then turquoise, then red.

7 Tie a large loop knot at each end of the string when you have finished threading, to stop the beads falling off. Your necklace is ready to wear.

Native American Homes

DURING THE WINTER months, the Inuit of the far north built their dome-shaped homes out of blocks of ice or with hard soil, wood and whale bones. Houses had to be adapted to their surroundings. Where wood was plentiful in the east, a variety of homes was built. The wikiup, or wigwam, was dome-shaped and made out of thatch, bark or hide, tightly woven across an arch of bent branches. Basic, rectangular thatched houses were built from a construction of chopped twigs covered with a mixture of clay and straw, or mud. Near the east coast, massive longhouses, up to 45m long, with a barrel-shaped roof, were made from local trees. Some tribes lived in different kinds of shelters depending on the season. The Plains Indians mostly lived in tipis (tents made of hide) or sometimes in earth lodges. The nearest to modern buildings were the homes of the Pueblos in the Southwest. These were terraced villages built of bricks made of mud. The Pueblo Indians also built round underground ceremonial chambers with a hidden entrance in the roof.

AT HOME
A Mandan chief relaxes with his family and dogs inside his lodge. Notice how a hole is cut in the roof to let out smoke from the fire and let fresh air in. Earth lodges were popular with Mandan and Hidatsa people on the Upper Missouri. The layout followed strict customs. The family would sleep on the south side, guests slept on the north. Stores and weapons were stored at the back. The owner of this home has his horse inside to prevent it from being stolen while the family is asleep.

HOMES ON THE PLAINS
The hides of around 12 buffaloes were used to cover a family tipi belonging to a Plains Indian. Tipi comes from a Siouan word meaning to dwell. Hides were sewn together and stretched over wooden poles about 8m high. When it became too hot inside, the tipi sides were rolled up. In winter, a fire was lit in the centre.

TOTEM POLE
Totem poles were usually found in the far northwest of the United States. They were carved out of wood, often from the mighty thuja (red cedar) trees. Tall totem poles were erected outside the long plank houses of the Haida people. These homes were shared by several families. The poles were carved and painted to keep a record of the family histories of the people inside. They were also sometimes made to honour a great chief.

EARTH LODGES

Mandan Indians perform the Buffalo Dance in front of their lodges. These were built by using logs to create a dome frame, which was then covered over with tightly packed earth.

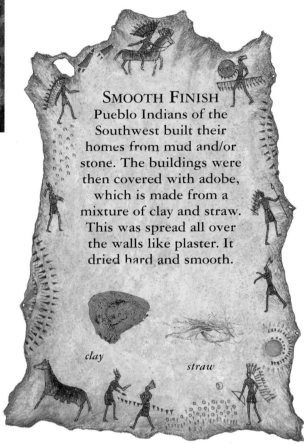

SMOOTH FINISH

Pueblo Indians of the Southwest built their homes from mud and/or stone. The buildings were then covered with adobe, which is made from a mixture of clay and straw. This was spread all over the walls like plaster. It dried hard and smooth.

clay

straw

LAYERS OF BRICK

This ruin was once part of a complex of buildings belonging to Pueblo Indians. Pueblo homes were often multi-storeyed with flat roofs. The floors were reached by ladders. Circular brick chambers were built underground. These were the kivas used for religious and ceremonial rites.

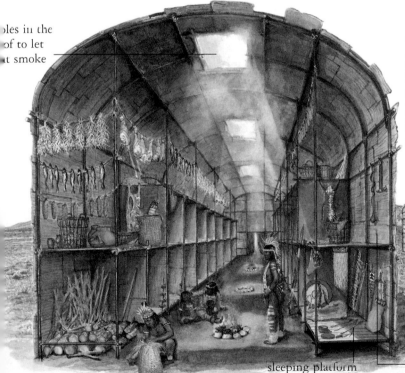

holes in the roof to let out smoke

sleeping platform

THE LONGHOUSE

Iroquois people of the Woodlands built long wooden houses. The frame was made of poles hewn from tree trunks with cladding made from sheets of thick bark. Homes were communal. Many families lived in one longhouse, each with their own section built around an open fire.

higher platform for storing food

Groups of longhouses were built together, sometimes inside a protective fence.

Home Life

Roles within the family were well-defined. The men were the hunters, protectors and tribal leaders. Women tended crops, made clothes, cared for the home and the sick, and prepared the food. The children's early days were carefree, but they quickly learned to respect their elders. From an early age young girls were taught the skills of craftwork and homemaking by their mothers, while the boys learnt to use weapons and hunt from the men. Girls as young as 12 years old could be married. Boys had to exchange presents with their future in-laws before the marriage was allowed to take place. At birth most children were named by a grandparent. Later, as adults, they could choose another name of their own.

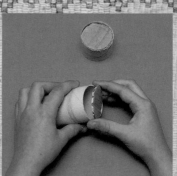

BONES FOR DINNER
This spoon was carved from animal bone. For the early family there were no metal utensils. Many items were made from bone, tusks, antlers or horns. Bone was also used to make bowls.

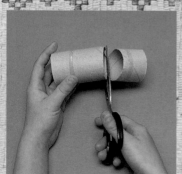

A DAY'S HUNTING
Blackfoot girls look on as men leave camp on a hunting trip. They are in search of bison. If the hunt is successful, the women will help skin the animals then stretch out the hide to dry. Buffalo skins were used to make tipi covers. Softer buckskin, from deer, was used for clothing.

HOLDING THE BABY
A woman holds her baby strapped to a cradleboard. Domestic scenes were often the focus of Indian crafts, reflecting the importance of family life.

MAKE A KATCHINA DOLL
You will need: cardboard roll, ruler, scissors, compasses, pencil, thick card, PVA glue, brush for glue, masking tape, paints in cream/yellow, green/blue red and black, paintbrush, water pot, red paper.

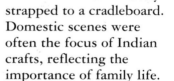

1 Take the cardboard roll and cut a section of about 4cm (or a third) off the top. This will form the head piece. The larger end will form the body.

2 Use the compass (or end of the cardboard roll) to draw four circles of 2cm radius on card. Then draw a smaller circle 1.5cm radius. Cut them all out.

3 Glue the larger circles to either end of both of the cardboard roll tubes. Leave to dry. Glue the smaller circle of card on top of one end of the longer roll.

ROLE PLAY

Children love to copy their elders, and this little Sioux girl is wearing an adult's large headdress. She is holding a favourite doll to pose for the picture. Playing with dolls taught girls about their future role as a carer. Boys enjoyed learning how to ride, shoot arrows and hunt.

FAMILY GATHERING

A Cree family in Canada enjoys a quiet evening around the fire. American Indian families were usually small as no more than two or three children survived the harsh life. However, a lodge was often home to an extended family. There could be two or three sisters, their families and grandparents under one roof.

Katchina dolls were made by the Hopi people to represent different spirits. This is the Corn katchina. Some parents gave the dolls to their children to help them learn about tribal customs.

BABY CARRIER

For the first year of its life, a baby would spend its time strapped to a cradleboard, such as this one influenced by the eastern Woodland tribes. It was also used by eastern Sioux, Iowa, Pawnee and Osage parents. A baby could sleep or be carried in safety while laced in its cradle, leaving the mother free to work. The board was strapped to the mother's back.

4 The smaller cardboard circle forms the doll's neck. Fix the small cardboard roll (the head) on top of the larger cardboard roll (the body) with glue.

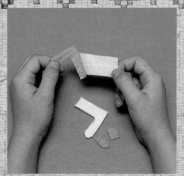

5 Cut two small L-shapes from card to form the arms. Then cut two small ear shapes from the card. Cover these shapes with masking tape.

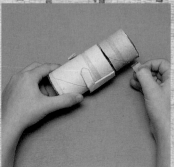

6 Glue the arms on to the body and the ears on to the sides of the head, so that they stick out at right angles. Paint the doll the colours shown above.

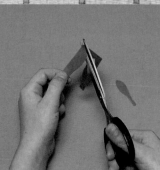

7 While the paint is drying, cut two small feather shapes from red paper. Glue these on to the top of the doll's head, so that they stick into the air.

29

Food and Farming

FROM THE NORTH AMERICAN Indians' earliest days, tribes have hunted, fished and gathered their own food. Archaeologists recently found evidence of a version of popcorn dating back to 4000BC. The area and environment tribes lived in determined their lifestyle. Inuit and coastal people would fish and hunt. Calusas in Florida farmed the sea, sectioning off areas for shellfish. Tribes on the Northwest Coast took their food from the sea and so had little reason to develop farming, although they did grow tobacco. For many tribes, however, farming was an important way of life and each developed its own agricultural skills.

The Secotan tribal name means an area that is burnt, referring to their method of setting fire to land to clear it for farming. They and other tribes on the fertile east coast planted thriving vegetable gardens. As well as the staple maize, squash and beans, they grew tomatoes, berries, vanilla pods and asparagus.

FOOD BASKET
The Apaches and other people in the Southwest are renowned for making beautiful baskets. They waterproofed them with melted pinon (tree nut) gum. Versatile basket bowls were used for storing corn and carrying or serving food.

COOKING OUTSIDE
This beehive-shaped structure is a traditional outdoor oven. It was used by the Pueblo and other people of the Southwest. A fire was lit inside the dome which heated stones placed all around the fire. The oven was used to bake corn bread or roast vegetables and meat.

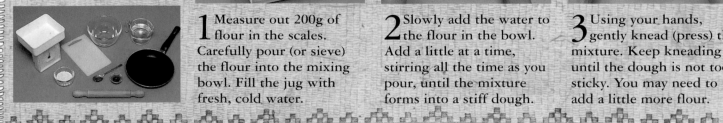

MAKE CORN CAKES
You will need: 200g corn tortilla flour or plain flour, weighing scales, sieve (optional), mixing bowl, cold water, jug, metal spoon, wooden or chopping board, rolling pin, frying pan, possibly a little oil for cooking, honey.

1 Measure out 200g of flour in the scales. Carefully pour (or sieve) the flour into the mixing bowl. Fill the jug with fresh, cold water.

2 Slowly add the water to the flour in the bowl. Add a little at a time, stirring all the time as you pour, until the mixture forms into a stiff dough.

3 Using your hands, gently knead (press) the mixture. Keep kneading until the dough is not too sticky. You may need to add a little more flour.

BAGGING WILD RICE

Two rice gatherers are sorting out their harvest of rice just as their ancestors would have done. Vast areas of wild rice grew on the shores of lakes and rivers of the eastern Woodlands. Men and women would gather the stalks, bend them over the edge of a boat and strike them with a blunt tool. The grains of rice would fall into the boat. They were then gathered in bags to dry in the sun.

THREE SISTERS

Maize (corn) was part of the staple diet of most tribes. It was grown as early as AD200. The two other important crops were squashes and beans. These three crops were known by the Iroquois as the Three Sisters.

squash

maize

mixed beans

PREPARING A MEAL

These Secotan people are sorting beans for a meal. Indians grew about 60 different types of beans. Most tribes were very hospitable and would prepare food to share.

FISH SUPPER

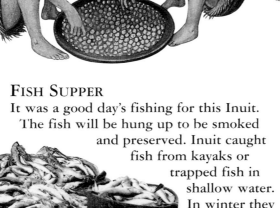

It was a good day's fishing for this Inuit. The fish will be hung up to be smoked and preserved. Inuit caught fish from kayaks or trapped fish in shallow water. In winter they fished through holes in the ice.

Corn cakes (or tortillas) were often eaten with beans and savoury food. They also taste delicious eaten with honey. Try them!

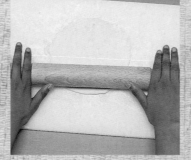

4 Sprinkle flour over the board. Take the dough from the bowl and knead it on the floured board for around 10 minutes. Leave it to stand for 30 minutes.

5 Pull off a small lump of dough. Roll it between your hands to form a flat round ball. Repeat this process until you have used all the dough.

6 Keep patting the dough balls until they form flat round shapes. Finish off by using the rolling pin to roll them into flat, thin cakes, also known as tortillas.

7 Ask an adult to come and cook them with you. Heat a heavy frying pan or griddle. Gently cook the cake until it is lightly browned on both sides.

Hunting

THE EXCITING BUT DANGEROUS TASK of chasing the herds began only after a buffalo dance had been performed. The first signs of the bison (the real name for American buffalo) were often tracks left in the earth. Hunters followed these until the herd was spotted in the distance. Early hunters stalked the animals on foot, which was very dangerous. They made an avenue out of rocks and bushes down which the bison were driven. This led to a buffalo jump where the animals were stampeded to the edge of a steep cliff to fall to their death. When the horse came, it made hunting easier though not always safer. A hunter had to ride in close to the herd, pick out a bison and drive it away.

Bison was not the only animal hunted. The rivers to the east were once rich in beaver, much favoured by fur traders, and tribes in California would hunt deer in the hills.

BUFFALO GRAVEYARD
The skulls were all that was left of the bison after a hunt. Meat was used for food, fat for glue and soup, and the hide became tipis and moccasins. Bladder and bones were made into cooking utensils, and the hair was used as stuffing.

HUNTING BEAR
This painting by George Catlin shows grizzly bears being speared by Plains warriors. Bears were sacred animals to many tribes, however, and believed to be guardian spirits. A warrior might paint symbols of the bear on his shield or red claw marks on his face for protection.

MAKE A SKIN ROBE
You will need: an old single sheet (or large piece of thin cotton fabric), scissors, tape measure or ruler, pencil, large needle, brown thread, felt in red, yellow, dark blue and light blue, PVA glue, glue brush, black embroidery thread (or string), red cotton thread (or other colour).

1 Take the sheet and cut out a rectangle 140cm x 60cm. Then cut out two 40cm x 34cm rectangles for the arms. Fold the main (body) piece in half.

2 At the centre of fold, draw a neckline 22cm across and 6cm deep. Cut it out. Roll fabric over at shoulders and stitch down with an overlapping stitch.

3 Open the body fabric out flat and line up the arm pieces, with the centre on the stitched ridge. Stitch the top edge of the arm pieces on to the body.

BUFFALO RUN

Hunters on horses rush at a bison trying to force it towards archers lying in wait. On a hunt, the first aim was to get all the animals to run in a circle. Then the hunters would surround them picking off individual animals until they had all the meat needed. If the bison stampeded, the chase went on.

FOOLING THE BUFFALO

Hunters have disguised themselves as wolves to creep up close to the bison. The skin masked the hunter's own body smell and they often tried to imitate a wolf's movements. It was essential to keep downwind because of the bison's keen sense of smell. However, the bison had very poor eyesight.

The North American Indians would have made their robes from buckskin. When the Europeans first spotted the natives wearing it, they could not work out what the pale, soft material was made from.

BUTCHERS AT WORK

A hunt is over and the tribe moves in to skin and butcher the kill. Often it was the women and elder children who handled the harvesting. The skin would carefully be taken off in one piece and used to make clothing. Meat would be prepared for a feast.

4 Fold the fabric in half again to see the shirt's shape. Now stitch up the undersides of the sleeves. The sides of the shirt were usually not sewn together.

5 Your shirt is ready to decorate. Cut out strips and triangles of felt and glue them on to the shirt. Make fringes by cutting into one side of a felt strip.

6 Make fake hair pieces by cutting 8cm lengths of black thread and tying them together in bunches. Wind red thread tightly around the top, as here.

7 Glue or sew the fake hair (or scalplocks) on to your shirt. You can follow the pattern we used as shown in the picture (top), or create your own.

The Mighty Bison

For generations, the native bison (or buffalo) provided the Plains Indians with most of life's essentials such as their food and housing materials. Although they hunted all year round, summer and autumn were the main buffalo seasons. During the summer months, large herds of thousands of animals came to the grass ranges to fatten up for winter. The arrival of the bison was marked by excited ceremonies before hunting began. The night after a successful hunt, a large feast was held with singing and dancing. A great deal of bison meat was eaten at the feast, but some had to be preserved for harder times. For this the meat was cut into narrow strips and hung over wooden racks to dry in the sun or over a fire. This is called jerky. Tougher meat was minced and mixed with bison fat and berries, a delicacy known as pemmican.

BUFFALO DANCE
Mandan men are getting themselves in the right mood for a hunt. Buffalo dances were held to bring the hunters good luck. Legend has it that the bison taught men their dance and chant. The Plains Indians believed in many spirits. They felt that if they prayed and chanted, the spirits would help them. The bull (male) head and hide robes were sacred objects worn by the shamans (medicine men) and those offering up prayers for the hunt.

OFFERING A PRAYER
A lone Indian stands on top of the hill. He is using the sacred skull of a buffalo to call upon the great spirit of Wakan Tanka to bring buffalo herds to the Great Plains. The Sioux believed their world was full of spirits that controlled the earth, the sun, the sky, the wind — in fact, everything. Wakan Tanka controlled all of the spirits.

HUNTER VERSUS THE BISON
A large bull (male) turns on his attacker. An average male weighed more than a tonne and stood more than 1.5m high at the shoulder. The lone rider is armed with a spear and guides his horse with knee pressure alone. A hunt was a chance for a warrior to prove himself. If he killed a bison, a hunter had the honour of eating the heart. The Indians believed that this transferred the bison's spiritual power to the hunter.

A HUNT GOES ON

The excitement of bison hunting is captured in this Blackfoot painting on a tipi lining. Pictures were used to record significant events in tribal life. They were painted on tipis or shields. The images described war exploits, good hunting trips or the family history. The bison here were probably eaten by the tribe.

STRETCHING THE HIDE

An Oklahoma man is stretching and tanning the hide in a traditional way. North American Indians stretched buffalo skin over a wooden frame or staked it out on the ground. First, the fat, flesh and fur had to be scraped away, then the skin was washed with a mixture of grease and water. Sometimes urine was used. Rawhide, the uncured animal skin with its fur scraped off, was used to make drums, shields and robes.

WILD AND FREE

In 1800 there were an estimated 60 million bison roaming the Plains. These numbers fell dramatically as European settlers moved further west. Around four million bison were slaughtered in just four years. They were hunted almost to extinction. In 1872, Yellowstone Park was the first conservation area set up to protect them.

HUNTING AS SPORT

Passengers on the Kansas Pacific Railroad shoot buffalo for sport. When railways were built in 1860 white settlers moved west of the Mississippi and on to the Plains. There, they came across bison. They did not understand the Indians' way of life and killed many animals. Later, the United States government encouraged white hunters to shoot herds. They thought that if the bison were destroyed, tribes would lose their livelihood and give up their land.

Storytelling

NORTH AMERICAN INDIANS LOVED storytelling. Many stories taught the children to respect nature and animals or described social behaviour. Stories were also a way of passing on tribal customs, rituals and religious beliefs. Some tribes considered it unlucky to tell tales of mythological events during the summer months. They looked forward to the long winter nights when they would gather in their tipis or lodges and huddle around the fire. Then, they listened to the storyteller who was often one of the elders. A story might recall past hunts and battles, or it could be a work of complete fiction, although the listener could never be sure as the tales were always embellished. This was especially true if the storyteller was from the Yuma. The Great Dreams of the Yuma were fantastical tales usually performed as plays and often based on tribal rituals and folklore.

SCROLL OF A SHAMAN
This is a fine example of a birchbark scroll. It is a Midewiwin (Grand Medicine Society) record of the Ojibwa. Most ceremonies were so long and complicated that a chart had to be made to remember all the songs and prayers in the right order. A document such as this was used to record the history and initiation rites of a tribe. Without it, knowledge of them might be lost forever.

STORY BEHIND THE PICTURES
A proud Mandan chief and his wife pose for a picture to be painted. It is not just the chief's headdress that reveals great prowess in battle. The painted skin displayed by the woman tells stories of the tribe's history. The war scenes show that the tribe has been involved in many victorious battles in the past. This group picture was painted between 1833 and 1835 by George Catlin. He was an artist whose paintings of North American Indians are themselves a form of storytelling. They are an important source of information about tribal lives, customs and dress, particularly as the Indians at that time did not write any books about themselves.

COLOURED SAND
Although many tribes made sandpaintings *(shown above)* it was the Navajo who developed the art. The painter trickled powders of yellow, white and red ochre and sandstone into patterns on the sand. Each picture described humans and spirits connected with creation stories and was usually used as part of a healing ceremony.

HEROIC TALES
The Sioux chief, seen at the bottom of this picture, must have been exceptionally brave as his headdress is very long. Painting warrior shields was an ancient art used to pass on tales of battle heroics. This shield may have been painted by one of the warriors involved. Shields were kept in the lodge and brought out when the warrior retold how brave he was. It would be given to his children to keep his memory alive.

WRITTEN IN STONE
These children are reading about the history of their ancestors in Colorado Springs. Stone Age North American Indians (the early Pueblo people) carved animals and designs on stone which told a little of their way of life.

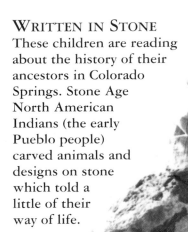

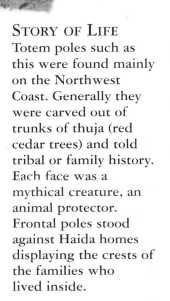

THE HISTORIAN
A young boy looks on as his father records tribal stories on dried animal hide. He is already learning the importance of recording the family history. Even in 1903, when this picture was painted, many tribes used picture writing, not the printed word of the white man.

STORY OF LIFE
Totem poles such as this were found mainly on the Northwest Coast. Generally they were carved out of trunks of thuja (red cedar trees) and told tribal or family history. Each face was a mythical creature, an animal protector. Frontal poles stood against Haida homes displaying the crests of the families who lived inside.

Myths and Legends

TRIBAL LIFE WAS FILLED WITH myths and famous tales. Legends of tribal ancestors, gods and spirits were handed down through the generations. Some of the greatest legends were told in song or dance at large gatherings. They were often connected with religious beliefs and many of the tales were an attempt to explain the origins of the tribes and the universe. The Haida, Snohomish and Quinault (of

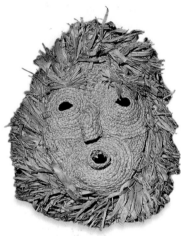

the Northwest Coast) believed that animals were the original inhabitants of the land. They thought that the coyote (a large wild dog) could take off its fur to reveal a man inside. It was the god Kwatee, who created humans from the coyote. The Iroquois believed in a sky woman and earth goddess called Ataensic. She died giving birth to twins. After her death, one of the twins created the world from her corpse. In Navajo mythology, a sea goddess known as White Shell Woman was in charge of water, and her sister was an earth goddess who made the seasons change each year.

BUSHY HEADS
Members of the Iroquois Husk Face Society wore this type of mask. They were said to have special healing powers and could handle hot ashes and rub them on the heads of patients. The masks were made of braided corn husk and nicknamed bushy heads.

LARGER THAN LIFE
The mighty Thunderbird was a powerful supernatural creature, seen here in a Haida wood carving. A flap of its wings was said to bring thunder, and lightning struck when it blinked. The Algonquins in the east called them Our Grandfathers. They could fight with other beings or grant mighty blessings.

MAKE A SPIRIT MASK
You will need: thick card, scissors, pencil, masking tape, newspaper, flour, water, bowl and fork for mixing, fine sandpaper, white and red acrylic paint, paintbrushes, water pot, bradawl, elastic, twine, PVA glue, brush for glue.

1 Cut out an oval piece of card, a little larger than your face. Make four 2cm cuts, two towards the top and two at the bottom, as shown above.

2 Overlap the cut bits of card and tape them down. This will create a 3-D shape to fit your face. Ask a friend to help mark holes for eyes and mouth.

3 Cut the eye and mouth holes then build up the nose, cheeks and mouth. Fold up bits of newspaper to make the right shapes and tape them into place.

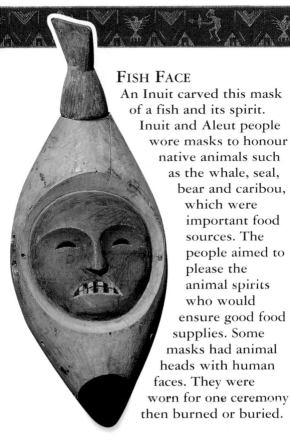

FISH FACE
An Inuit carved this mask of a fish and its spirit. Inuit and Aleut people wore masks to honour native animals such as the whale, seal, bear and caribou, which were important food sources. The people aimed to please the animal spirits who would ensure good food supplies. Some masks had animal heads with human faces. They were worn for one ceremony then burned or buried.

SPIRIT MASK
This scary face is an Inuit mask. Creatures in the spirit world were recreated in masks and so the masks were felt to be alive. Ordinary people wore masks during ceremonies, but shamans wore them more often. A mask carved by a shaman would give him spiritual powers to heal sick people.

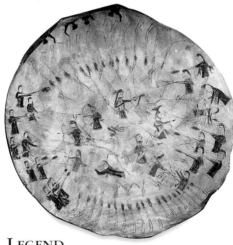

SUMMONING SPIRITS
The god of lightning is represented by this katchina doll. Hopi, Zuni and other Pueblo Indians carved many katchina dolls. They were no ordinary dolls, a katchina was a guardian spirit. The Hopi believed the spirits lived in the mountains. They came down on the winter solstice (shortest day of the year) and stayed until the summer solstice (longest day).

LEGEND IN THE MAKING
The pictographs on this Sioux war shield show that the tribe had fought in a huge battle. They are surrounded by the US Cavalry – the figures around the edges. Many scenes of legendary battles have been recorded on shields.

Your mask follows the design of a False Face Mask of the Iroquois. The wearer was a member of a False Face Society and used it during ceremonies to cure the sick.

4 Mix up a paste of flour and water. Tear bits of newspaper into small strips, dip them into paste and cover the mask with them. Make 2–3 layers.

5 Leave the mask to dry in a warm place. When dry, smooth it down with sandpaper. Coat in white paint then red, or just several layers of red.

6 When dry, add more detail using white paint. Make a hole on either side using a bradawl. Tie a piece of elastic to each side to fit the mask on your face.

7 Take the twine and dampen it slightly then untwist it so you have straw-like strands. Dry them out and glue them to the mask to create hair.

Craftwork

NORTH AMERICAN INDIANS were expert craftsmen and women. Beautiful pots have been found dating back to around 1000BC. The people of the Southwest were renowned for their pottery. Black and white Mimbres bowls were known as burial pots because they were broken when their owner died and buried along with the body. Baskets and blankets were the other most important crafts. The ancient Anasazis were known as the basket-making culture because of the range of baskets they produced. Some were coiled so tightly they could hold water. The Apaches coiled large, flat baskets from willow and plant fibre, and the Paiutes made cone baskets, which were hung on their backs for collecting food. All North American Indians made use of the materials they had to hand such as wood, bark, shells, porcupine quills, feathers, bones, metals, hide and clay.

BASKET WEAVER
A native Arizona woman is creating a traditional coiled basket. It might be used for holding food or to wear on someone's head. Tlingit and Nootka tribes from the Northwest Coast were among those who wore cone-shaped basket hats.

POTTERY
Zuni people in the Southwest created beautiful pots such as this one. They used baskets as moulds for the clay or coiled thin rolls of clay around in a spiral. Afterwards, they smoothed out the surface with water. Birds and animals were favourite decorations.

DRILLING WALRUS TUSKS
An Inuit craftsman is working on a piece of ivory. He is using a drill to etch a pattern. The drill bit is kept firmly in place by his chin. This way, his hands are free to move the bow in a sawing action, pushing the drill point into the ivory.

MAKE A TANKARD
You will need: air-drying modelling clay, board, water in pot, pencil, ruler, cream or white and black poster paints or acrylic paints, fine and ordinary paintbrushes, non-toxic varnish.

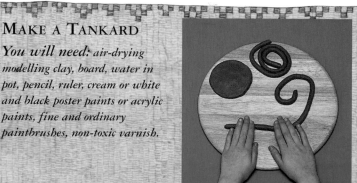

1 Roll out a round slab of clay and press it into a flat circle with a diameter of about 10cm. Now, roll out two long sausage shapes of clay.

2 Slightly dampen the edges of the clay circle. Place one end of the clay sausage on the edge of the circle and coil it around. Carry on spiralling around.

3 Continue coiling with the other clay sausage. Then, use your dampened fingers to smooth the coils into a good tankard shape and smooth the outside.

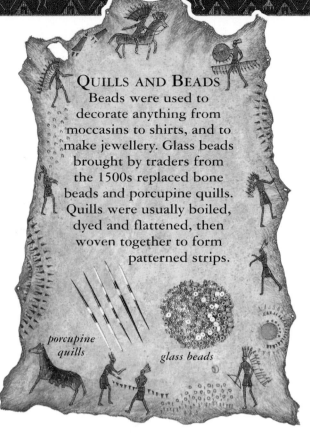

QUILLS AND BEADS

Beads were used to decorate anything from moccasins to shirts, and to make jewellery. Glass beads brought by traders from the 1500s replaced bone beads and porcupine quills. Quills were usually boiled, dyed and flattened, then woven together to form patterned strips.

porcupine quills

glass beads

TALKING BLANKET

It could take half a year for a Tlingit woman to make one of the famous Chilkat blankets. She wove cedar bark fibre and mountain goat wool with her fingers. The Tlingits said that if you knew how to listen, the blankets could talk.

FRUITS OF THE LOOM

Striped blankets were the speciality of Indians in the Southwest. This Hopi woman is using an upright loom made from poles. Pueblo people were the first North American Indians to weave like this.

Each tribe had its own pottery designs and colours. These geometric patterns were common in the Southwest.

4 Roll out another, small sausage shape of clay to make a handle. Dampen the ends and press it on to the clay pot in a handle shape. Leave to dry out.

5 Using a sharp pencil, mark out the design you want on your jug. You can follow the traditional indian pattern or make up your own.

6 Using poster paints or acrylic paints, colour in the pattern on the mug. Use a fine-tipped brush to create the tiny checked patterns and thin lines.

7 When the paint is dry, coat your mug in one or two layers of non-toxic varnish using an ordinary paintbrush. This will protect it.

Games and Entertainment

AS HARD AS LIFE WAS, the North American Indians always found time to relax by playing games and entertaining themselves. There were games of chance and gambling and games of skill. Games of chance included guessing games, dice-throwing, and hand games where one person had to guess in which hand his opponent was hiding marked bones or wooden pieces. Archery, spear throwing and juggling were favourite games to improve hunting skills and there was a variety of ball and stick games, such as lacrosse. Children also loved to swim and take part in races. In the north, the girls and boys raced on toboggans. Active pastimes like these helped to develop skills a North American Indian needed to survive, such as strength, agility, bravery and stamina. Ritual foot races were also of ceremonial importance. By running, the Indian could supposedly help the crops grow, bring rain and give renewed strength to the sun.

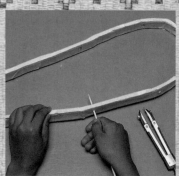

TEAM GAMES
The Ball Game of the Creek, Seminole, Cherokee and Choctaw people was similar to lacrosse. The Indians used two sticks, while in lacrosse, one is used. Cherokees called it *little brother of war*, and to the Choctaw it was *stickball*.

SNOW FUN
These Inuit children are enjoying a toboggan ride in the snow. They are well wrapped up in animal skins. Iroquois adults played Snow Snake to see how far a lance could be slid on ice.

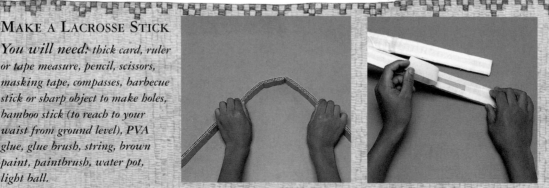

MAKE A LACROSSE STICK
You will need: thick card, ruler or tape measure, pencil, scissors, masking tape, compasses, barbecue stick or sharp object to make holes, bamboo stick (to reach to your waist from ground level), PVA glue, glue brush, string, brown paint, paintbrush, water pot, light ball.

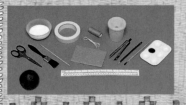

1 Measure, then cut a strip of card 120cm x 3cm. Fold it gently at the centre to make a curve (Or cut two 60cm x 3cm pieces and tape them together).

2 Cover the card completely with masking tape. Start from the edges and work round, keeping the bent shape. Cover both sides.

3 Use a compass to mark two points from the centre of the bend, 10cm apart, then two, 10cm from these and two more 10cm down. Use a stick to make holes at these points.

GAME OF THE ARROW

Plains tribes enjoy a spot of target practice. A stationary target was made of wood, grass or bark. A more adventurous game for the archer was to throw a bundle into the air and try to shoot an arrow into it before it came down. This was a favourite with the Mandan, who tried to shoot several arrows into the air at the same time from one bow.

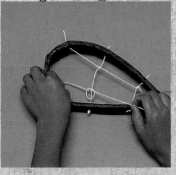

The aim of the game of lacrosse is to get the leather ball between two posts to score a goal. It is a bit like hockey, but instead of hitting the ball, it is scooped up in the net of the curved stick or racquet.

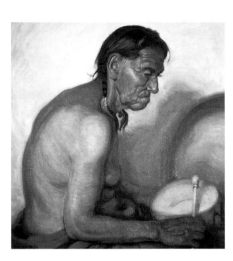

KEEPING THE BEAT

Songs and dance were essential during ceremonies. They inspired visions among listeners who often chanted to the rhythmic beat.

wooden flute

Plains drum

drum and beater

rattle

MUSIC TIME

Instruments were made from everyday materials. Drums were the most important. There were various types of flat or deep drums, mostly made from rawhide (untreated buffalo skin) stretched over a base of carved wood. Reed flutes were sometimes played by Sioux men when they were courting their future wives.

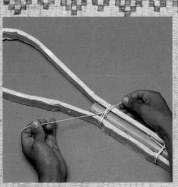

4 Glue the ends of the card strip to the top of the bamboo stick leaving a loop (as shown above). Tie string around the outside to keep it in place.

5 Pinch the card together at the end of the stick, just under the loop. Tie it tightly with string and trim the ends. Now paint the stick brown.

6 When the paint is dry, thread two pieces of string horizontally between the two sets of holes on the sides of the loop. Knot them on the outside.

7 Now thread the vertical strings. Start at the holes at the top of the frame and tie the string around both horizontal strings. Tie the ends. Use a light ball.

Contact with Europeans

THE VIKINGS WERE THE first Europeans to discover the existence of North America. It was other explorers arriving around 500 years later, however, who created the most impact. These Europeans claimed the land for their own countries, setting up colonies of settlers. They eventually forced many North American Indians from their homelands, killing thousands in the process. When Christopher Columbus landed in the Bahamas in 1492, he set about claiming the land for Spain. Fellow Spaniard Ponce de León landed in Florida in 1512, while Hernando Cortés had conquered the Aztecs in Central America by 1521. Tales of mountains of gold in the Southwest brought a Spanish expedition headed by Vasquez de Coronado. He encountered Apache, Hopi, Pawnee and Wichita Indians. He never did find gold. Sadly, the European explorers and colonists never regarded the Indians as equals. They tried to force tribes to change their lifestyles, beliefs and even to adapt their traditional crafts to suit European buyers.

EARLY VISITORS
Erik the Red, the Viking king, sailed to Greenland around 982AD. He was probably in search of new trading partners. His son Leif later sailed to Newfoundland and established a settlement at a place now called L'Anse aux Meadows. A trade in furs and ivory was set up with northern Europe.

SETTING SAIL
Columbus and his crew prepare to set sail from Spain in 1492 in search of a trade route to India. He never reached Asia but landed on San Salvador in the Bahamas. The Arawaks there thought that Columbus and his men came from the sky and greeted them with praise. Columbus set about claiming the islands for the Spanish Empire, making many of the natives slaves.

A Distant Land

This map from around 1550 shows a crude European impression of North America. Henry II of France ordered Descallier, a royal cartographer (map maker), to make a map of what middle and North America looked like. The French were keen to gain land there for themselves. Jacques Cartier, a French navigator, spent eight years exploring the St Lawrence River area. He made contact with Huron communities. He wrote and told the king that he hoped the Indians would be "easy to tame".

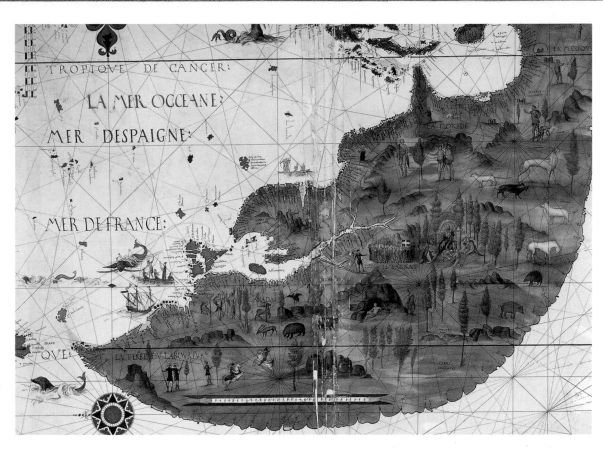

Man with a Mission

A Plains Indian views a missionary with suspicion. Eastern tribes were the first to meet French missionaries whom they called Black Robes. In California, Indians were forced to live and work in Spanish mission villages.

Say a Little Prayer

Young Indian girls dressed in European clothes have been separated from their families and tribal customs. Europeans could not understand the North American Indians' society and religious beliefs. They wanted to convert them to Christianity, by force if necessary. In many areas, children were taken away from their people and sent to white boarding schools, given European names and taught European religion, language and history

European Settlers

FROM 1500, NORTH AMERICA was visited by the English, French and Spanish in increasing numbers, each establishing colonies to expand their empires. It was mostly the British and the French who stayed. At first their settlements were on the east coast and in eastern Canada, but gradually they explored further inland, meeting with more and more tribes. Europeans brought diseases previously unknown to the Indians. The smallpox epidemic of 1837 almost wiped out the Mandan tribe. Fewer than 200 people survived, from a tribe that had once numbered over 2,500. The colonists continued to push out the North American Indians. In the 1760s to 1780s, colonists fought for independence from their empires. In 1783 the United States was officially recognized as being independent from Britain. The US government wanted to move eastern tribes west of the Mississippi River. They bought the Louisiana Territory in 1803 for 15 million dollars from France. This doubled the size of the US and marked the end of French rule. It didn't stop there – they continued to push their frontiers west.

LEADING THE WAY
Sacawagea, a Shoshoni girl, guides US captains Meriwether Lewis and William Clark from Mississippi to the Pacific coast, in 1804. It took them almost one year. President Thomas Jefferson asked them to map out the land from the Mississippi River to the Rockies. This helped to pave the way for settlers to move to the far west.

ROLLING ACROSS THE PLAINS
From around 1850, wagon trains were signs that times were changing for the Plains tribes. Although settlers had been living in North America for around 300 years, they had mostly remained on the east coast. The US government encouraged white families to move inland.

SOD HOUSE
This is a fine example of a soddy, a house literally made from sod, or turf, cut out of the ground. Settlers had to build homes from whatever material was to hand. Life was hard for the children, they had to do chores, such as feeding chickens. If they were lucky, they went to school.

NEW TOWN

Plains Indians watch a train steaming into a new town. Land was sacred to the tribes who called it their Earth Mother. The settlers thought that the tribes wasted their land and wanted to build towns and railways on it. At first the federal government just took land for settlers. Later, they bought millions of acres of Indian land in various treaties (agreements), using force if the Indians did not agree.

PANNING FOR GOLD

A man is sifting through sand in search of gold. When gold was discovered in late 1848 in California, it started the Gold Rush. Thousands of immigrants came to the west coast from all over the world. The sheer numbers forced the tribes off their land.

TRAIN ATTACK

Plains warriors attack a train crossing their hunting grounds. The Plains tribes had always been fiercely defensive of their territory. Now they turned on the new invaders. More and more settlers were encouraged to move on to the Plains. In the 1860s railways were constructed across Indian lands. These were built over sacred sites and destroyed buffalo hunting grounds which were essential to the tribes' livelihood. Attacks on settlers, trains and white trading posts became more frequent.

Horse Culture

THERE WERE HORSES ROAMING wild in America during prehistoric times, but they had died out by the Ice Age. The Spanish reintroduced the horse to North America in the early 1500s when they brought the animals over on ships. As the Spanish moved north of Mexico further inland, more tribes came into contact with the horse. It was forbidden by Spanish officials to trade in horses, but gradually tribes obtained them one way or another. To go on a horse-stealing raid was counted as a great honour. The arrival of the horse on the Plains had a dramatic effect on tribal life. It meant that they could expand their hunting area, and made hunting bison far easier. It also meant that greater loads could be carried or pulled by horses, including much larger tipis. By 1700, the Crows traded horses with the Colombian Plateau tribes of the Nez Perce, Cayuse and Palouse. The Cayuse became renowned for breeding a strong type of horse, which bears their name. The Palouse were also very good at breeding horses and their name was given to the Appaloosa breed favoured by the Nez Perce tribe. Tribes treated the animals with respect and there was often a special bond between a warrior and his horse.

PLAYING THEIR PART
Horses feature prominently among the many pictures painted by Plains Indians on deer and buffalo skins. On this Blackfoot buffalo robe, the horses are shown helping warriors to victory in battle and transporting people and property to new camp sites. In a short time, horses had become crucial to the Plains people's way of life. They could never go back to life on foot.

WILD SPIRIT
An Indian catches a horse that was roaming wild on the Plains. The new owner would spend weeks teaching the animal to accept a rider on its back. More usually, Indians would catch horses in raids on other tribes or settlers' camps. Life on the Plains produced a strong and hardy pony.

HORSE RUSTLING
These Indians appear to be on the lookout. Some tribes bred horses to trade, others were not so honest. The Comanche raiders in Texas would steal horses from other Texans or Mexicans and then trade them to friendly tribes.

OFF OUR LAND

A chief stands on his horse to emphasize the point he is making. The white man is probably marvelling at the Indian's ability to stay upright. Plains Indians were famed for their showmanship and riding skills. The chief's saddle blanket is made from tanned buffalo hide. Most Indian riders used blankets rather than saddles. Many tribes, such as the Crow, made bridle ornaments and beaded saddlebags while others painted symbols on the horses.

TAMING THE HORSE

These boys are attempting to break in a wild horse. When horses were first acquired by tribes, only brave young men and women rode them, although they were used to carry goods. It took about a generation for horses to be accepted.

A TEST OF HONOUR

This Blackfoot Indian could be on a horse raid. Stealing horses from another tribe was one way a warrior could prove that he was brave. The raids were not thought of as a crime, more an expression of honour. The Comanche were regarded as the best horsemen and were feared by other tribes and white settlers alike.

COVETED HAIR

Horsehair adorns the head of this Iroquois False Face Mask. American Indians made use of everything around them. Horsehair was used for a variety of things. It could be braided together to make rope. It was used as stuffing in a cradle to give the baby some comfortable padding. It could also add the final decoration to an eagle feather headdress.

Markets and Trade

NORTH AMERICAN INDIANS HAD a long tradition of trading. The Hopewell civilizations of about AD200 brought metals and other materials to their centres around the Ohio valley. The Calusas in southern Florida had a vast trade network both inland and across the sea to the Bahamas and Cuba. Many people would travel long distances to buy and sell goods at a regular meeting place. Although some tribes used wampum (shell money), most swapped their goods. People from settled villages exchanged agricultural products such as corn and tobacco for buffalo hides, baskets or eagle feathers from nomadic tribes. When European traders arrived, in the 1600s, they exchanged furs and hides for horses, guns, cotton cloth and metal tools. Early trading posts such as the Hudson's Bay Company were built by whites. These posts were usually on rivers which could be reached easily by canoe.

WORDS OF A WAMPUM
A Mohawk chief, King Hendrick of the League of Five Nations, was painted on a visit to Queen Anne's court in London in 1710. He holds a wampum belt made from shells. These were made to record historic events such as the formation of the League of Five Nations of the Iroquois.

BASKETS FOR GOODS
Crafts, such as this Salish basket, were sometimes traded (or swapped) between tribes, and later with Europeans. Indians particularly wanted woollen blankets while European traders eagerly sought bison robes.

COLONIAL TRADERS
A native hunter in Canada offers beaver skins to colonial fur traders in 1777. They would probably have been made into beaver hats. Beaver fur was the most important item the Woodlands tribes had to trade, as competition between European nations for animal skins was fierce. This trade was partly to blame for many tribal conflicts. The Iroquois were renowned beaver hunters who ruthlessly guarded their hunting territory.

SHELL SHOW

A Plains Indian is holding up a wampum belt decorated with shells. The belts were usually associated with the Iroquois and Algonquian tribes who used them to trade, as currency, or to record tribal history. Quahog clam shells were strung together to make a long rectangular belt with patterns showing tribal agreements and treaties. Even colonists used them as currency when there were no coins around.

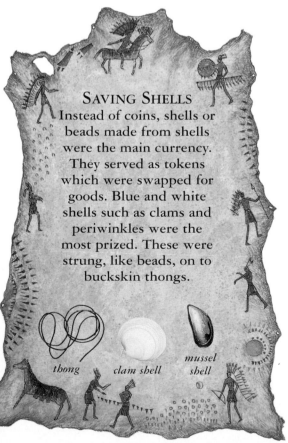

SAVING SHELLS

Instead of coins, shells or beads made from shells were the main currency. They served as tokens which were swapped for goods. Blue and white shells such as clams and periwinkles were the most prized. These were strung, like beads, on to buckskin thongs.

thong *clam shell* *mussel shell*

TRADING POSTS

North American Indians would gather in the Hudson's Bay trading post. In return for bringing in pelts (animal furs), the Indians would be given European goods. Many would be useful such as iron tools and utensils or coloured cloth. Firearms and liquor traded from around 1650 did the tribes more harm than good. As trade increased, more trappers and hunters frequented the trading posts. Later, some of the fur trade posts became military forts and attracted settlers who built towns around them.

Warriors and Warfare

MOST WARS BETWEEN TRIBES were fought over land or hunting territory, and later over horses. As Europeans began to occupy more land, many tribes fought to stop them. Each tribe had warriors, known as braves. There were military societies within the tribe like the Cheyenne Dog Soldiers whose job was to protect the tribe. Warriors would paint both themselves and their horses for spiritual protection. A white stripe across a Blackfoot warrior's face meant vengeance. In the 1700s, Plains tribes traded guns with the Europeans, but they felt that blasting their tribal enemies lacked honour. Instead, warriors developed a way of fighting without killing. A warrior had to get close enough to strike his enemy with a long stick known as a counting coup, then escape unhurt. Each act of bravery earned an honour feather to be tied to the stick.

HEAVY HANDS
Crude tomahawks such as this date back to the Stone Age, but were still used by Plains warriors in the late 1800s. War clubs made from local rocks were vicious weapons, as was the wooden gunstock club which had a large spike sticking out.

WEAPONS
This tomahawk dates back to around 1750 and once belonged to an Iroquois warrior. Before they acquired firearms, warriors had a variety of weapons of war. They used the bow and arrow, knives, or long lances, as favoured by the Comanches from Texas.

HORSEMANSHIP
This Plains warrior displays excellent horse skills. He is riding on the side of his horse, holding on with just one foot tucked over the horse's back. This shields him from harm while his hands are free to thrust his spear. Sioux warriors believed that horses fought with their rider in battle. If a warrior died, Apaches would often kill his horse and bury it with its master's body.

MAKE A SHIELD
You will need: thick card, ruler, pencil, scissors, PVA glue, glue brush, masking tape, two 35cm strips of balsa wood dowel 1cm in diameter, white cotton (or other fabric) approx 40cm square, red, black and cream or yellow paints, paintbrush, water pot, brown felt.

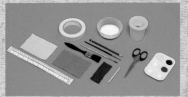

1 Cut two strips of thick card measuring 2.5cm x 118cm. Glue them together to give a double thickness. Then bend them to make a circle.

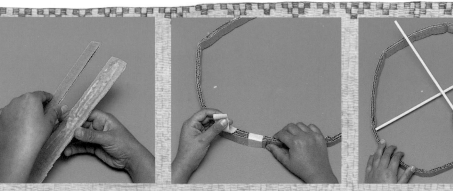

2 Glue and tape the ends together to form a circle, with about 4cm overlapping. The diameter should be approximately 36cm. Leave to dry.

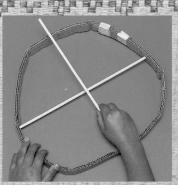

3 Cross and glue the two dowel sticks together at right angles. Glue both to the frame, one from top to bottom, one horizontally. Leave the base to dry.

WARRIORS' TOOLS

Local hard rock such as obsidian, slate or flint was shaped into knives, arrowheads, spears and axes by striking it with another stone. Bone tools were used to chip away flint to make sharp, fine points. Metal arrowheads were also made from scrap tin from the Europeans.

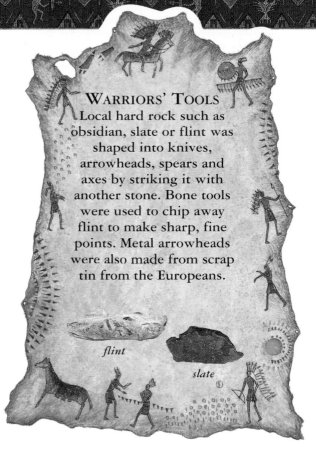

flint

slate

HERO'S FRIEND

The shield was one of the warrior's most prized possessions. He felt it gave him both spiritual and physical protection. Skin from the bison's neck was used to make it, as this was the toughest part of the animal. It could be decorated with symbols and feathers or scalps.

DRESSED FOR BATTLE

Chief Quanah Parker of the Comanche is wearing his war costume. Each tribe had a war chief who was in charge of planning attacks. He was not usually the leader of the people, but had proved himself to be a brave warrior in battle. Chief Parker led his followers in battles throughout Texas. They fought against the United States in the Red River War of 1874–75. His mother, Cynthia Parker, was a white captive of the tribe.

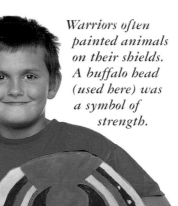

Warriors often painted animals on their shields. A buffalo head (used here) was a symbol of strength.

4 Lay the fabric flat. Using the frame as a guide, draw round it to make a circle 2.5cm wider than the frame. Cut out the circle.

5 Draw a pattern on the fabric, then paint it. A simple, bold pattern works best, or copy our shield and paint a buffalo head. Allow the paint to dry.

6 Stretch the fabric over the frame, keeping the pattern centred. Glue down the edges all round. Paint the edges red (background colour) to neaten them.

7 Cut a strip of brown felt measuring around 2.5cm x 40cm. Glue the ends to the top and bottom edges of the shield at the back. This is the armband.

53

War and Defeat

FROM 1775 TO 1783, COLONISTS fought for independence from Britain. Some Indians remained neutral in the Revolutionary War, some took sides. The Iroquois League of Nations at first did not want to be involved in a white man's quarrel. They had, however, allied with the British against the French in other European wars. The League was split and eventually most of the tribes supported the British. In 1777, they ended up fighting some of their own people, the Oneidas, who had sided with the Americans. The United States gained independence in 1783. With new strength, the US started pushing for more land and introduced the Indian Removal Act of 1830. The aim was to relocate eastern tribes west of the Mississippi River on to reservations (areas set aside for Indians). The Choctaws were the first tribe to be relocated in 1830, to Oklahoma. They were followed by the Chickasaws, Creeks and Seminoles. Many long and bitter battles were fought as the Indians struggled to keep their homelands. Much reservation land was neither as fertile nor productive as the old tribal land, and some tribes faced starvation.

WILD WEST
There were many conflicts between US soldiers and different tribes, such as this attack in the 1800s. Some attempts at peaceful talks were made. However, military records show that between 1863 and 1891, there were 1,065 fights.

TRAIL OF TEARS
The heartbroken Cherokee nation is being forced to leave its homelands in 1838–39. During the trek west, rain and snow fell and soldiers made them move on too quickly. It is estimated that almost 4,000 Cherokees died from exhaustion and exposure.

MAKE ANKLE BELLS
You will need: white felt, ruler, pencil or felt tip pen, scissors, strong thread, needle, 10 to 16 small bells – between five and eight for each anklet.

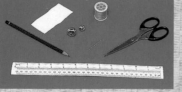

1 Cut out two strips of white felt 75cm x 5cm. Measure and mark a line across the felt strips, 24cm in from one end. Do the same at the other end.

2 Now make a series of marks in the middle section of the strips. Start 3cm away from one line, then mark every 3cm. This is where the bells will go.

3 Create the fringing at each end of the anklet. Do this by cutting into both ends of the band up to the pencilled lines. Do the same for the other anklet.

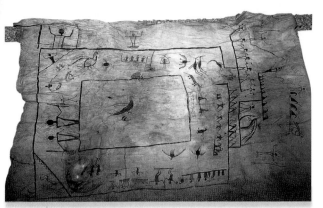

WAR BUNDLE

This buckskin was used to wrap a personal war bundle. It has been painted with the Thunderbird and other supernatural beings for spiritual protection. A bundle might carry a warrior's medicine herbs or warpaint.

THE SHIELD SURVIVED

This warrior's shield belonged to a Dakota (Sioux) warrior in the late 1800s. It may have been used in the Battle of Little Bighorn. The Sioux tribes fought in many battles with the US around that time. In 1851 their lands were defined by a treaty. Then, when gold was found in Montana, gold hunters broke the treaties by travelling through Sioux land, and war raged again.

THE END OF GENERAL CUSTER

The Battle of Little Bighorn, in 1876, is counted as the last major victory of the North American Indian. Custer's entire 7th Cavalry was defeated by Sioux sub-tribes, after they attacked an Indian village. Sadly, this made US soldiers even more brutal in their dealings with tribes.

WAR DANCE

Sioux warriors are performing a war dance. During the dance a medicine man would chant and ask for spiritual guidance and protection for warriors going into battle. Other dances were performed after a battle.

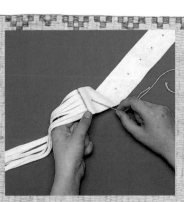

4 Thread a large needle with strong, doubled and knotted thread. Insert the needle into the fabric and pull through until the knot hits the fabric.

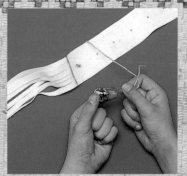

5 Thread the needle through the bell and slip the bell up to the felt. Then insert the needle back into the felt very near to the place it came out.

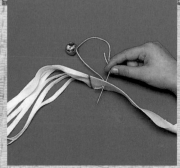

6 Push the needle through and pull tight. Knot the end (opposite side to the bell) to secure and cut away the excess thread. Repeat with the other bells.

The bells of the North American Indians were sewn on to strips of animal skins. They were tied around the ankles or just under the knees, for ceremonial dances.

Customs and Beliefs

NORTH AMERICAN INDIANS DID NOT believe in a single god. They believed that the changing seasons and events surrounding them were caused by different spirits. To them, everything in the world had a soul or spirit which was very powerful and could help or harm humans. Spirits had to be treated with respect, so prayers, songs, chants and dances would be offered to please them. The most important spirit to the Sioux was Wakan Tanka, the Great Spirit or Great Mysterious, who was in charge of all other spirits. The Navajo believed in the Holy People. These were Sky, Earth, Moon, Sun, Hero Twins, Thunders, Winds and Changing Woman. Some tribes believed in ghosts. Western Shoshonis, Salish (Flathead) people and Ojibwas considered ghosts to be spirit helpers who acted as bodyguards in battle. The leader of ceremonies was the shaman (medicine man) who conducted the dances and rites. He also acted as a doctor. The shamans of California would treat a sick person by sucking out the pain, spitting it out and sending it away.

CHARMED LIFE
A whale's tusk was used to carve this Inuit shaman's charm. Spirits called tuneraks were thought to help the angakok, as the Inuit shaman was called, in his duties. The role of shaman was passed from father to son. In Padlimuit, Copper and Iglulik tribes, women could also be shamans.

BEAR NECESSITIES OF LIFE
This shaman is nicknamed Bear's Belly and belonged to the Arikara Plains tribe. Shamans were powerful, providing the link between humans and spirits. After years of training, they could cure ill health, tell the future or speak to the dead.

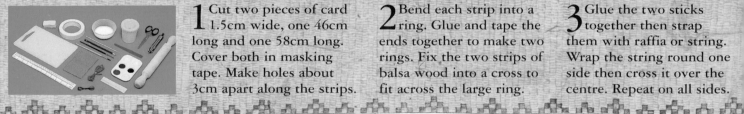

MAKE A RATTLE
You will need: thick card, pencil, ruler, scissors, masking tape, compasses, PVA glue, brush, two balsa wood strips 2–3cm wide and about 18cm long, raffia or string, air-drying clay, barbecue stick, cream, black, orange/red and brown paint, paintbrushes, water pot, black thread, needle.

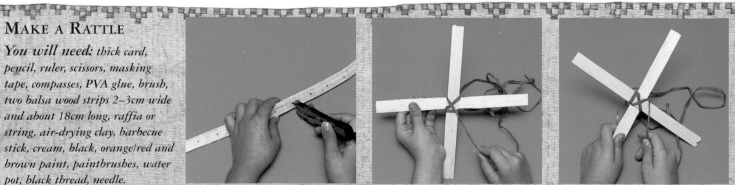

1 Cut two pieces of card 1.5cm wide, one 46cm long and one 58cm long. Cover both in masking tape. Make holes about 3cm apart along the strips.

2 Bend each strip into a ring. Glue and tape the ends together to make two rings. Fix the two strips of balsa wood into a cross to fit across the large ring.

3 Glue the two sticks together then strap them with raffia or string. Wrap the string round one side then cross it over the centre. Repeat on all sides.

THE HAPPY COUPLE
Menominee people of the Woodlands made these dolls to celebrate the marriage of a couple. The miniature man and woman were tied face to face to keep husband and wife faithful. Dolls feature in the customs of many tribes, not least the Hopi and Zuni of the Southwest. Their katchina dolls are spirits shown in the form of animals, humans or plants.

NATURAL REMEDY
Medicine men used a variety of potions to cure ills. These included herbs and plants such as nettles, yarrow, willow, jimson-weed and tobacco or red ants. They might be fed to the sick patient, put on the skin or waved around them to ward off evil.

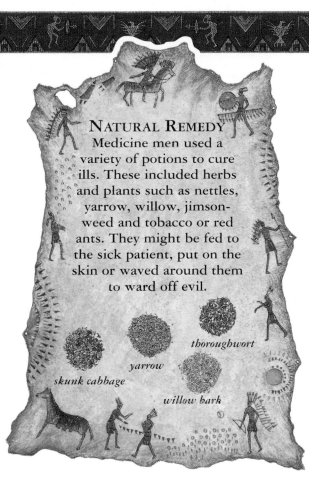

thoroughwort

yarrow

skunk cabbage

willow bark

MEDICINE BAGS
Crystals, animal parts, feathers and powders made of ground up plants and vegetables might be inside these bundles. They were used to make cures and spells by a shaman (medicine man) of the Winnebago tribe from the Woodlands.

SACRED BIRD
Rattles such as this Thunderbird rattle from the Northwest Coast were considered sacred objects and carved with the images of spirits. They were made of animal hoofs, rawhide or turtle shells, and filled with seeds or pebbles. Some were hand held, others were put on necklaces.

Rattles were an important part of any ceremony. In some tribes only shamans could hold one.

4 Glue the two card rings on to the cross, as here. The larger ring sits on the outer ends of the cross. The smaller one is roughly 1–2cm inside of that.

5 Roll out the modelling clay to a 1cm thickness. Cut out 20 to 30 semicircle shapes to resemble penguin beaks. Use a stick to make a hole at one end.

6 When the beaks are dry, paint them cream. Leave to dry. Paint the tips black then paint red or orange stripes. Next, paint the two rings brown.

7 Thread the black cotton through the hole in a painted beak, then tie it through one of the holes in the rings. Repeat with each beak, filling both rings.

The Sweat Lodge and Other Rites

SWEATING PURIFIED THE BODY and mind according to North American Indians. The Sioux called it "fire without end". The sweat was one of the most important and ancient of all North American religious rituals. They were among the first people to use heat to cleanse the body. But for tribe members, it was not simply a question of hygiene. The sweat lodge rite was performed before and after other ceremonies to symbolize moving into and out of a sacred world. Warriors prepared their spirits before the Sun Dance ceremony by taking a sweat bath. This was a dance to give thanks for food and gifts received during the year, and often featured self-mutilation. Sweats were also taken to purify the body and as a medical treatment to cure illness. They were often one of various customs, such as rites of passage from childhood to adulthood. A young boy who was about to make his transition into warrior-life was invited to spend time with the tribe's males. They would offer him the sacred pipe which was usually smoked to send prayers. This was called Hunka's ceremony and showed the tribe's acceptance that the boy was ready. Some warrior initiation rites were brutal – such as the Mandan's custom of suspending young men by wooden hooks pierced through their chest, or scarring them, known as Okipa. Both girls and boys prepared for passing into adolescence by spending time alone and fasting (not eating).

STEAM AND SMOKE
A holy man, such as this Pima shaman, would be in charge of sweats. Prayers and chants were offered and the sacred pipe was passed around each time the door was opened.

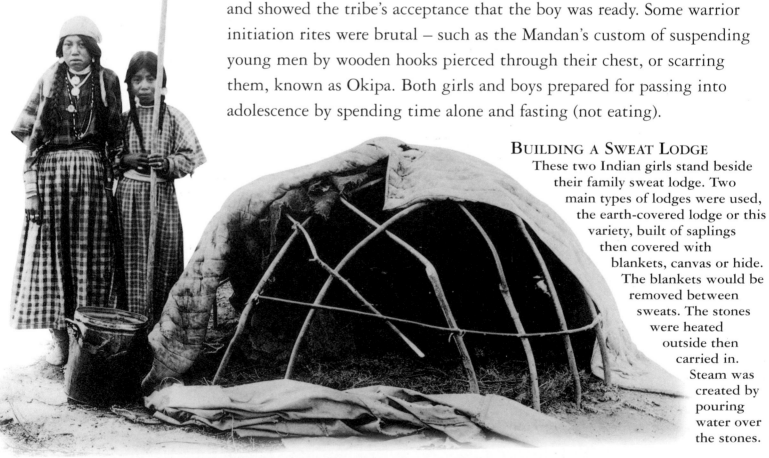

BUILDING A SWEAT LODGE
These two Indian girls stand beside their family sweat lodge. Two main types of lodges were used, the earth-covered lodge or this variety, built of saplings then covered with blankets, canvas or hide. The blankets would be removed between sweats. The stones were heated outside then carried in. Steam was created by pouring water over the stones.

BATHS IN EARTH

An Indian crawls out from an earth-covered sweat lodge for air. Six to eight people could sit around the hot stones inside, depending on the size of the sweat lodge. Males and females would both take part in sweats but it was customary to do so separately. In some tribes, families built their own family lodges and some larger sweat lodges were also used as homes or temples. Sticks and wood formed the frame. This was covered in mud or clay. The fire would be built in the lodge causing a dry heat. It was dark, stuffy and hot, similar to the saunas used in Europe. However, a sweat lodge was used to cleanse the spirit as well as the skin.

CLEANSED AND REFRESHED

Herbs, such as sweetgrass and cedar, were often put on the hot stones inside a sweat lodge. When the water was poured over the stones, the smell and essence of the herbs were released into the lodge with the steam. Herbs helped to clear the nasal passages. They could also be selected to treat particular ills. As the heat from the steam opened up the skin's pores, the herbs could enter the body and work at the illness or help purify the spirit. Sweating removed toxins (poisons in the body) and, the Indians believed, forced out disease.

GROWING UP

A young Apache girl is dressed up for a modern tribal ceremony. The lives of North American Indians were filled with rituals to mark each milestone in a person's life or important tribal events. There were ceremonies for birth, for becoming an adult or to mark changing seasons.

INSTRUMENTS TELL A STORY

This Tsimshian rattle has been involved in many ceremonies. Tribes had a vast amount of ceremonial objects, from rattles to headdresses, clothing and wands. Their decorations were usually of spiritual significance. In some tribes, the frog was respected since it would croak when danger was near. Others believed that their long tongues could suck out evil. A frog also stars in creation myths of the Nez Perce.

Sacred Dances

DANCING WAS AN IMPORTANT PART of North American Indian life. Some of the sacred dances were performed before or after great events such as births, deaths, marriages, hunts or battle, but it meant more than a big party. The Green Corn Dance was held annually to bring in the Creek New Year and celebrate agricultural growth. The Arikara Bear Dance hoped to influence the growth of maize and squash crops. Dancers often wore costumes. The Cheyenne Sun dancers painted their upper body black (for clouds) with white dots (for hail). The Assiniboine Clown dancers often danced and talked backwards and wore masks with long noses.

DOG DANCE
A Hidatsa warrior from the Crazy Dog Soldier Society performs the Dog Dance to thank spirits for his strength. His headdress is made from magpie tail feathers with a crest of turkey tail feathers. The Hidatsa on the Missouri had many societies, including the White Buffalo Society, a women's group. The White Buffalo Woman was a mythical spirit.

SNOWSHOE DANCE
The Snowshoe Dance was performed after the first snow each winter by some Woodlands tribes. To the Indians, snow meant the passing of a year. People would speak of something happening two snows ago. Winter was a hard time, food was scarce with few animals around to hunt. The dance asked spirits for help to survive.

MAKE A DANCE WAND
You will need: white paper, ruler, pencil, scissors, black and cream paint, paintbrush, water pot, 8 x 20cm lengths of balsa stick 3mm thick, PVA glue, glue brush, compasses, thick card, red and orange paper, a stick 75cm long and 1cm thick, string.

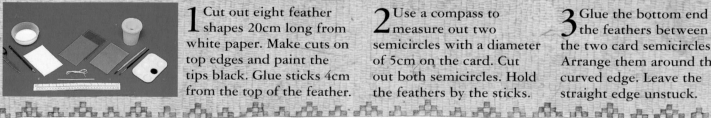

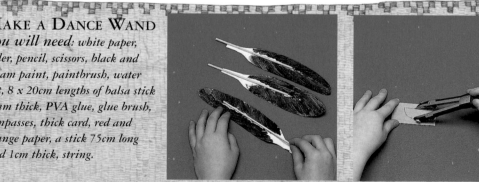

1 Cut out eight feather shapes 20cm long from white paper. Make cuts on top edges and paint the tips black. Glue sticks 4cm from the top of the feather.

2 Use a compass to measure out two semicircles with a diameter of 5cm on the card. Cut out both semicircles. Hold the feathers by the sticks.

3 Glue the bottom end of the feathers between the two card semicircles. Arrange them around the curved edge. Leave the straight edge unstuck.

PREPARING FOR WAR

Only men joined in war dances such as this Sioux ceremony. Warriors were preparing themselves for conflict. They hoped to gain favour with the spirits who would protect them from their enemies. Deer tails and feathers might hang on dance wands, but lances and spears had more grisly decorations. They displayed trophies of war such as the head of the enemy or scalps (a patch of skin and hair cut from an enemy in battle).

NATIVE KILT

This buckskin apron (or kilt) was once worn by a shaman during ceremonial dances. It is decorated with a picture of a beaver, a native North American animal. The beaver is this shaman's totem, a spirit helper. The spirit would be called upon to give the dancer strength to drive away sickness and evil spirits, and bring luck.

Ceremonial wands were carried during dances. Sometimes just one huge eagle feather or an animal tail hung from the top.

4 Draw and cut out 12 6cm long feathers from the red and orange paper. Make eight more red ones, 2.5cm long. Make feathery cuts into the top edges.

5 Divide the 6cm feathers in two and glue them to each end of the long stick. Secure them with string tied around the stick and bottom of feathers.

6 Paint the semicircles cream, then dry. Bend back the two straight edges. Place the flaps either side of the centre of the stick. Glue them firmly in place.

7 Glue the smaller red feathers to the outside tips of the black feathers (one on each). Leave to dry. Your wand is ready, so let the dance begin.

North American Indians Today

RECORDS SHOW THAT BY 1900 the American Indian population north of Mexico was down from between 2.5 and 3 million, to 400,000. Today the figure is in the region of 1,750,000. From the 1800s, many North American Indians were moved by the United States government from their homelands to areas of land known as reservations. In Canada, the Indian lands are called reserves. There are several hundred of these, smaller in size than the US reservations, but the Indians were not moved. About 300 US federal reservations still exist today, some for a single tribe, others as home to a number of groups. In the 1900s, Indians became more politically active, helped by political groups such as the American Indian Movement (AIM). Tribes began seeking compensation for lost land. The Cherokees were awarded 15 million dollars for lands they had lost. Many reservations are now governed by the tribes. Some are run by a council with an elected chief. In a way, it is similar to traditional tribal society. However, the US government still has control over much surviving Indian land. Since 1970, tribes have been allowed to run their reservation schools and to teach children their ancestral history.

MODERN CEREMONIES
This couple are joining other American Indian descendants at a powwow (tribal gathering). The meetings are popular because of a recent surge of interest in the culture of the tribes. Powwows give the people a chance to dress in traditional costume, speak their native language and learn more about their tribal history.

TRIBAL PROTEST
In July 1978 these American Indians walked for five months to Washington from their reservations to protest to Congress. At protest meetings, leaders read from a list of 400 treaties, all the promises that the United States had broken. For years, many tribes tried to get back land taken from them. In 1992, Navajo and Hopi tribes were given back 1.8 million acres of their land in Northern Arizona to be divided between the tribes.

SODA BAR STOP
A Seminole family enjoy sodas in 1948 in a Miami store. Tribes gradually adapted to the American ways of life, but some kept their own customs and dress. Seminoles were forced from Florida to Oklahoma in 1878. Almost 300 refused to leave the Everglades and around 2,000 live there today.

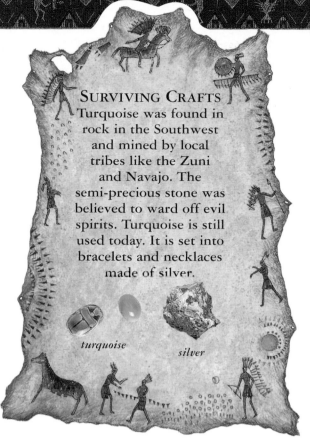

THE TOURIST TRAIL
A traditional Inuit scene of snowshoes propped outside an igloo. Most people in Alaska and Greenland live in modern, centrally heated homes. However, the ancient skills of building temporary shelters from ice bricks still survive. They are passed down to each generation and occasionally used by hunters or tourists keen to experience North American Indian customs.

CHEERLEADING CHIEF
Dressed in full ceremonial costume, this North American Indian helps conduct celebrations at a football stadium. It is a way of raising awareness of the existence of tribes. The cheerleading is not far removed from a war chief's tribal role of encouraging warriors in battle.

STITCHING THE PAST
Traditional American Indian crafts are still made today. The method of curing hides has remained the same. No chemicals are used during the tanning process and the scraping is still done by hand. However, styles of the crafts had already changed to suit the European market in the 1600s when traders brought in new materials.

TRADITIONAL SKILLS
An Indian craftsman produces beautiful jewellery in silver and turquoise. Zuni and Navajo people were among the finest jewellery makers in this style. Other tribes, such as the Crow, are famous for their beadwork.

Arctic Peoples

The first Europeans to visit the far north found a hostile environment where survival seemed almost impossible. Yet Arctic groups of people had lived there for thousands of years. The Inuit of North America and Greenland lived mainly by hunting wild animals such as seals, whales and foxes, while to the east, the peoples of Siberia and Scandinavia mostly lived by herding reindeer.

An Ancient History

T HE ARCTIC is one of the wildest, harshest places on Earth. Arctic winters are long, dark and bitterly cold. A thick layer of ice and snow blankets the region for much of the year. Today, people from developed countries can survive in the Arctic with the help of the latest technologies, such as modern homes, petrol-driven snowmobiles and clothes made from warm man-made fibres. Yet the original Arctic inhabitants thrived in this icy world for thousands of years. They did not have any of these modern aids to help them.

Arctic peoples used the natural world around them to survive. Slain animals provided food, skins for clothes and shelter and bones for tools and weapons. Although early Arctic peoples left no written records behind them, archaeologists can piece together the history of these people from finds such as tools and the remains of old buildings. The modern descendants of these early residents continue to carry on some of the traditional ways of Arctic living.

EARLY PORTRAIT
This portrait of three Arctic hunters was painted in the 1800s by one of the first European explorers to visit the Arctic. Drawings made by early European explorers, along with other records they collected, are a good source of information about the history of the region.

TRADITIONAL SKILLS
A girl from Arctic Russia learns to soften reindeer skins, using a method that has been used by her ancestors for thousands of years. Ancient Arctic peoples developed a way of life that was so successful that it has changed very little over the generations.

TIMELINE 10,000BC–AD1600

Humans have lived in the Arctic region for thousands of years. The huge periods of time involved, and the lack of written records, mean that the dates given to some of the earlier events are only approximate.

10,000BC and earlier Groups of people in Arctic Russia and Scandinavia live a nomadic life, following huge herds of reindeer that they hunt for food.

10,000BC During the last Ice Age, nomadic peoples move into North America from Siberia, travelling across a bridge of dry land that linked the two landmasses.

Small Tool People harpoon used to hunt sea mammals

3000–1000BC The Small Tool People live on the shores of the Bering Strait. Later they move east into Arctic Canada and Greenland. They use tools, such as needles to make clothes, and harpoons to hunt food.

1000BC–AD1000 The Dorset People dominate the North American Arctic. They use sea *kayaks* to hunt sea mammals, such as seals and walruses. The Dorset People live a nomadic life during the summer months, travelling in small groups and living in skin-covered tents.

Dorset culture hunter in his kayak

10,000BC

5000BC

1000BC

ANCIENT SITES

Archaeologists unearth the remains of a prehistoric house in the Canadian Arctic. Excavations of these early settlements reveal tools, weapons and other important objects. This information can tell archaeologists a lot about the lives of early Arctic people.

TOOLS AND WEAPONS

This harpoon point was carved from a walrus tusk. In ancient times, Arctic people were skilled at many crafts. Numerous tools and weapons were shaped from the bones of slain animals.

KEEPING TRADITIONS ALIVE

Inuit children get ready for a traditional feast of seabird meat, prepared according to an age-old recipe. Feasts and festivals such as these help to keep ancient Arctic traditions alive, preserving them for future generations of Inuit to enjoy.

FROZEN WORLD

The Arctic region lies at the far north of our planet. Its limit is the Arctic Circle, an imaginary line encircling the Earth at a latitude of 66 degrees north. Much of the Arctic region is a vast, frozen ocean, surrounded by the northernmost parts of Asia, Europe, North America and Greenland. All areas inside the Arctic Circle experience at least one day each year when the Sun shines all day and night, and at least one day when the Sun never rises.

---

knife of Dorset origin

AD1–AD1000 In winter, the Dorset people live in snow-house communities and use knives and clubs to kill seals at their breathing holes on the sea ice. During the later Dorset period, they develop artistic abilities. Many of the objects they make are used for magic, such as wooden masks. Around AD1000 the climate becomes warmer, which leads to the extinction of many of the Dorset people.

AD983 Viking warrior Erik the Red establishes a colony in Greenland.

Viking colony established in Greenland

AD1000–1600 The Thule People take over from the Dorset People. They live in stone and turf huts. They use *kayaks* and *umiaks* to hunt bowhead whales, and kill land animals, such as reindeer and musk oxen.

AD1570 onwards European sailors begin to explore the coast of Arctic Canada and also the seas north of Siberia. They come in search of whale oil, furs and wealth, and to find new sea routes to Asia.

Thule People continue to prosper until 1600

AD1000   AD1500   AD1600

The Arctic World

THE ICY WORLD of the Arctic holds traces of some very ancient civilizations. Indeed, archaeologists have found tools and weapons dating back to around 20,000BC. In prehistoric times, Arctic Russia and Scandinavia were inhabited by nomadic (wandering) peoples. They followed huge herds of reindeer, hunting the animals for their meat and fur. During the last Ice Age, more than 12,000 years ago, some of these nomads travelled from Asia to North America, crossing a bridge of land that once linked the two continents. Some settled in Arctic North America, while others moved to the warmer climate of the south.

Around 3000BC, a group called the Small Tool People lived around the coasts of Alaska. These people carved beautiful tools and weapons from bones and teeth. They made spears to hunt game and needles to sew animal skins into warm clothing. By 1000BC, another group called the Dorset People had come to dominate Arctic North America. They roamed the coastal waters in sea canoes, hunting seals and walruses. Two thousand years later, a third group, the Thule People, took over from the Dorsets. The Thule lived in houses built of turf and stone, used sledges pulled by dogs to travel over the ice and hunted huge bowhead whales.

The first Europeans to contact the Arctic peoples were the Vikings in AD983. From the late 1500s, Europeans came to the Arctic in increasing numbers. Until about 1800, life in the Arctic had changed very little for thousands of years. After that time, it began to alter much more quickly.

Extent of summ...

Nenet camp

Saami with Reindeer

EUROPE

TIMELINE AD1600–AD1900

AD1600–AD1800 European whaling ships visit the Arctic to hunt whales in the spring. The whaling industry booms until the 1800s.

whale hunting in the Arctic

trading furs with the Inuits

AD1720 Russian explorers map Siberia and cross from Asia to Alaska.

AD1720s onwards Russian merchants begin to trade with Arctic groups in Alaska. European merchants begin to trade for furs in northern Canada.

AD1720s Greenland is colonized by Denmark.

AD1750s onwards Christian missionaries arrive in North America and build schools and churches. They work to convert the local people to their religion. They discourage the work of shamans and undermine local peoples' faith in the spirit world. Many local people convert to Christianity.

wooden cross

AD1600   AD1700   AD1750   AD18

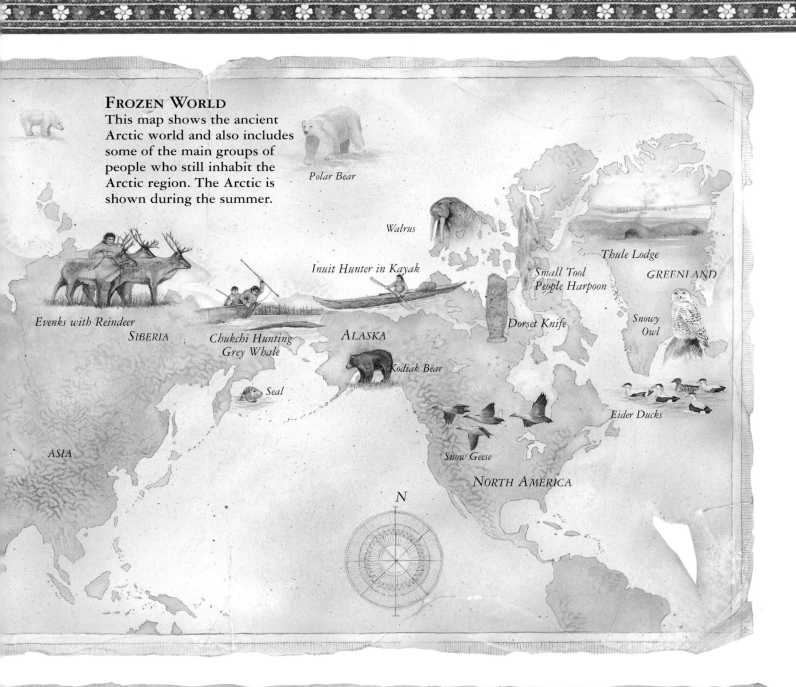

FROZEN WORLD

This map shows the ancient Arctic world and also includes some of the main groups of people who still inhabit the Arctic region. The Arctic is shown during the summer.

Polar Bear

Walrus

Inuit Hunter in Kayak

Thule Lodge

Small Tool People Harpoon

GREENLAND

Evenks with Reindeer

SIBERIA

Chukchi Hunting Grey Whale

ALASKA

Dorset Knife

Snowy Owl

Seal

Kodiak Bear

ASIA

Eider Ducks

Snow Geese

NORTH AMERICA

N

Hudson Bay trading certificate

AD1820 The Hudson's Bay Trading Company, a British business, is set up in the Canadian Arctic. It soon controls the fur trade and a vast area of northern Canada. Native people trade skins for European items, such as rifles.

AD1867 Russia sells Alaska to the United States.

AD1870s Whaling declines in the Arctic, due to overhunting by European whalers.

AD1880–AD1890s A gold rush starts at the Yukon River and Klondike in Alaska. Many new settlers also move to the American Arctic. Gold is discovered in Siberia, and soon coal is mined there as well.

Alaska becomes part of the United States

AD1900s onwards European missionaries convert increasing numbers of Arctic peoples to Christianity. As the influence of southern nations increases, life in the Arctic changes more quickly. The people of Arctic America, Europe and Asia are made subject to their nations' laws.

the lure of gold was the main reason for the mass settlement of Arctic America and Russia

AD1850

AD1900

Peoples of the North

THE ARCTIC IS HOME to many different groups of people. These groups are the descendants of ancient races who have lived in these frozen lands for thousands of years. Each group has its own distinctive way of life, culture and language.

The Inuit are the most northerly group in the Arctic, living on the coasts of North America from Alaska through Canada to Greenland, and on the tip of eastern Asia. Many Inuit still follow the traditions of their ancestors, harpooning seals, walruses and other sea creatures. The peoples of Arctic Europe and Asia live farther south. The Saami, also called the Lapps, come from Scandinavia. Many Saami continue to herd reindeer for food. Northern Russia is home to more than 20 Arctic peoples. Groups such as the Chukchi, Evenks, Nenets and Yakut herd reindeer and also hunt game, just as their ancestors did before them.

CHUKCHI

A Chukchi man rests on one ski, which is covered in moose hide. The Chukchi came from northeastern Siberia, the part of Russia closest to North America. Traditionally, they have closer links with the Inuit than with any other group from Arctic Asia.

SAAMI

A Saami, or Lapp, man from Norway cuddles his son. The Saami were well-known for their colourful, traditional clothing, decorated with bright bands of red, yellow and blue woven ribbon. The Saami still live in Scandinavia but many have adopted a modern lifestyle.

TIMELINE AD1900–AD2000

AD1909 US explorer Robert Peary is the first to reach the North Pole, with the help of Inuit teams.

AD1917 After the Russian Revolution, the Soviets take power in Russia. The communist system is imposed in Siberia and throughout the new Soviet Union.

Robert Peary at the North Pole

a radar station in the middle of the Arctic

AD1939-1945 During World War II, army bases are set up throughout the Arctic.

AD1945-1980s As World War II ends, the Cold War begins between the Soviet Union and the West. Radar stations are set up across the Arctic to warn of missile attack. Gradually new communities grow up around these bases.

AD1968 Rich fields of oil and gas are discovered at Prudhoe Bay in Alaska. Mining increases in the Arctic, leading to pollution and the loss of some traditional hunting and herding grounds.

oil power station

AD1900   AD1930   AD1960   AD19

EVENK

An Evenk man and woman show off their tame reindeer. These are draft animals, which means they are used for pulling sledges. In the frozen lands of northern Siberia in Russia, Evenks depend on reindeer for meat and for their hides, which are used to make warm clothing.

INUIT

This modern Inuit hunter's breath has frozen onto his beard. The Inuit used to be called Eskimos. This American Indian word means "eater of raw meat". However, most Inuit use the term *Inuit,* which means "the people". One Inuit man is called an Inuk.

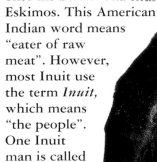

NENET

This Nenet girl is dressed in a warm coat made from reindeer skins. Nenets live over wide areas of Russia. Traditionally, these people live as nomads, travelling with the reindeer herds as they moved across the frozen Arctic wastes.

AD1977 Inuit and other Arctic peoples hold the first Inuit Circumpolar Conference. Arctic groups begin to organize, claiming traditional lands and demanding a say in their own affairs.

AD1979 Greenland wins home rule from Denmark.

the national flag of Greenland

seabird killed by an oil spill

AD1986 A fire at the nuclear power plant at Chernobyl in the Ukraine spreads radiation across the Arctic, polluting the reindeer pastures of the Saami and other Arctic herders.

AD1989 The wreck of the oil tanker *Exxon Valdez* pollutes the coast of Alaska and kills thousands of seabirds, otters and other creatures.

AD1990 Nunavut, a large territory in northern Canada, is awarded to the Inuit.

AD1999 The homeland of Nunavut is finally handed over to the Inuit.

modern day Inuit on a motorized snow scooter

AD1980   AD1990   AD2000

71

A Frozen Land

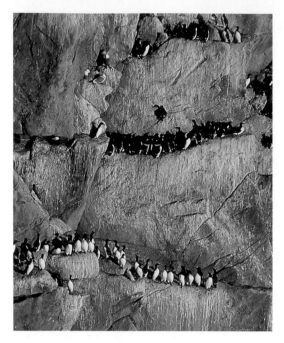

THE ARCTIC is one of the coldest places on our planet. Freezing winter weather lasts for eight or nine months of the year. Summers provide a brief break from these harsh conditions. The polar regions – the Arctic in the north and the Antarctic in the far south – are so cold because the Sun never shines directly over them. Instead, it hangs low in the sky. The ice and snow also help to keep the temperature low because they reflect sunlight back into space.

Most of the Arctic region is actually an ocean, topped by drifting sheets of ice. In winter, most of the ocean surface freezes over. Temperatures on land are almost always colder than in the water. Greenland, the landmass nearest to the North Pole, is covered by a thick ice cap all year round. Further south, the areas of Asia, Europe and North America that lie within the Arctic Circle are mainly tundra – vast areas of barren, treeless lowlands. South of the tundra, a belt of dense, evergreen forests called the taiga dominates.

SUMMER VISITORS
In spring, birds, such as these guillemots, migrate to the Arctic in huge numbers. The guillemots nest on crowded cliff edges, to lay eggs and raise their young. Other birds nest in open tundra. As the harsh winter weather sets in, the birds move south again. Many Arctic peoples hunted summer visitors such as these.

ICY LANDSCAPE
The Inuit village of Moriussaq in northern Greenland is covered by ice and snow for much of the year. In summer, temperatures rarely rise above 10°C. In winter, they often drop to −40°C. Throughout the Arctic region, the winter cold is so intense that the ground remains permanently frozen. This permanently frozen ground is known as permafrost. It may reach as deep as 600 metres in northernmost areas of the Arctic, such as Greenland and Siberia.

USEFUL PLANTS

Arctic peoples used the plants found in the region in many different ways. Some were eaten. For example, the leaves of the Arctic sorrel and the bark of the Arctic willow are rich in vitamins. Purple saxifrage yields a sweet nectar.

Purple saxifrage

Arctic willow

Arctic sorrel

WATERLOGGED SOIL

In the short Arctic summer, lakes, ponds and streams litter the surface of the Siberian tundra. In winter, the ground is permanently frozen. As summer approaches, however, the top layer of soil thaws. Water cannot penetrate the frozen layer below, so pools of water collect at the surface.

SPRING BLOOMS

In spring, Arctic plants, such as this yellow marsh saxifrage, quickly blossom. Flowering plants are found even in the far north of the Arctic. Many have special features that help them to cope with the bitterly cold conditions.

MIDNIGHT SUN

The midnight Sun lights up the pack ice covering the Arctic Ocean. The Sun never sets in the high Arctic during summer. In winter, it never rises, and the Arctic is a dark place. This is because the Earth tilts at an angle as it revolves around the Sun. In summer, the Arctic region leans towards the Sun, but in winter it tilts away.

NORTHERN LIGHTS

The northern lights or aurora borealis fill the skies over the Northwest Territories of Canada. The northern lights are an amazing display of red, yellow and green lights often seen in Arctic regions. They are caused by particles from the Sun striking Earth's atmosphere at the North Pole, releasing energy in the form of light.

Travelling with Reindeer

SOME ARCTIC PEOPLES have long depended on the reindeer. This large mammal is found throughout the frozen Arctic region. In North America, where reindeer are known as caribou, wild herds roam the land in search of food. In Europe and Siberia, they have been domesticated (tamed) for hundreds of years. In ancient times, the Saami, Nenets, Chukchi and other Arctic groups depended on the reindeer as a source of food. These people used reindeer skins to make tents and warm clothes. They also shaped the bones and antlers into tools and weapons.

Many Arctic animals are migratory creatures, which means they travel in time with the changing seasons. Reindeer are no exception. In spring, huge herds move north towards the shores of the Arctic Ocean. They spend the summer grazing the tundra pastures. In autumn, they journey south again to spend the winter in the sheltered forests of the taiga. In the past, the Saami and Nenets travelled with the reindeer, moving the beasts on so they did not graze the pastures bare. Some of their descendants still live the same nomadic life.

TENDING YOUNG DEER
A Saami herdsman lifts a newborn calf. Reindeer calves are born in May and June, following the herd's migration to northern tundra pastures in the spring. Just a few hours after birth, most newborn calves are strong enough to stand up and walk.

REINDEER FOOD
Reindeer moss carpets the forest floor in Labrador, Canada. Reindeer moss is the main source of food for reindeer, since it is found beneath the snow in winter. In summer, a wider variety of plants is available for the reindeer to eat.

ROPING REINDEER
A Saami herder uses a modern rope lasso to catch a reindeer from the herd. In the past, Saami herdspeople used reindeer hide to make their lassos. Saami families owned herds of between 200 and 1000 animals. The size of the herd was an indication of the family's wealth.

ARCTIC ADAPTATIONS

A Chukchi herdsman checks his reindeer during a light snowstorm. Reindeer are well adapted to life in the harsh environment of the Arctic. They are warm-blooded mammals, and they must keep their bodies at a constant temperature to survive. A thick layer of insulating fur helps to keep each animal warm. Reindeer also have "heat exchangers" in their muzzles to warm the air they breathe in. Reindeer have broad hooves that help prevent the animals from sinking into the deep snow and becoming stranded.

FENCED IN

A Saami herder uses a long, billowing cloth to drive his animals into a fenced corral. Reindeer herds were driven into corrals to check their health and to decide which animals were the best to kill. The herder also saw if he had another herder's reindeer.

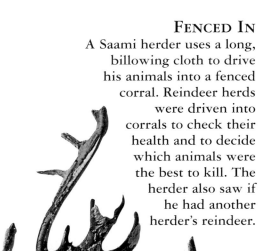

PACK LEADER

Traditionally, reindeer herds were led by tame deer wearing bells. Many Arctic Siberians kept male and female animals in separate groups.

VALUED ANIMAL

Reindeer were extremely useful animals. They provided meat, and their blood and milk were drunk. Reindeer hides were used to make clothes, bedding and rough shelters. Bones and antlers were shaped into harpoons, needles and other tools and weapons. Even the animal's sinews (tendons) were used as sewing thread.

milk

antler

hide

Settlements and Homes

TENT LIFE
A Nenet herder loads up a sledge outside his family's chum in preparation for another day's travel across Siberia. Chums were convenient, light and easy to assemble and dismantle. Some Nenets still live in chums, as their ancestors have done for generations.

M OST ANCIENT ARCTIC GROUPS lived in small villages containing a few families at most. The villages were spread out over a wide area, so each group had a large territory in which to hunt. In winter, the Inuit, Saami and other groups lived in sturdy houses built partly underground to protect them from the freezing conditions above. In summer, or when travelling from place to place, they lived in tents or temporary shelters.

In Siberia and parts of Scandinavia, groups such as the Nenets did not settle in one place. Their homes were lightweight tents, called chums in Siberia, made up of a framework of wooden poles and covered with animal skins. These chums could withstand severe Arctic blizzards and kept everyone warm inside when temperatures were icy.

BUILDING MATERIALS
A deserted building made from stone and whalebone stands on a cliff in Siberia. Building materials were scarce in the Arctic. In coastal regions, people built houses with whalebones and driftwood gathered from the beach. Inland, houses were mainly built with rocks and turf.

ARCTIC DWELLING
This illustration shows a house in the Alaskan subarctic with a portion cut away to show how it is made. Houses such as this one were buried under the ground. People entered by ladder through the roof.

MAKE A NENET TENT
You will need: 3 blankets (two at 2 x 1.5 m and one at 1.2 x 1.2 m), tape measure, string, scissors, 10 bamboo sticks (nine 180 cm long and one 30 cm long), black marker, black thread, a log or stone.

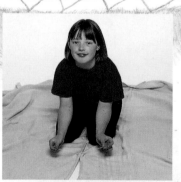

1 Cut small holes 10 cm apart along the shorter sides of the two large blankets. Thread a piece of string through the holes and tie the string together.

2 Cut a 60-cm length of string. Tie the 30-cm-long stick and a black marker 55 cm apart. Use the marker to draw a circle on the smaller blanket.

3 Tie four bamboo sticks together at one end. Open out the sticks onto the base blanket. Place the sticks on the edge of the circle so they stand up.

BONY BUNKER

Whalebone rafters arch over the remains of a home in Siberia. Part of the house was often built underground. First, the builders dug a pit to make the floor. Then they built low walls of rocks and turf. Long bones or driftwood laid on top of the walls formed sturdy rafters that supported a roof made from turf and stones.

MAKING WINDOWS

An old stone and turf house stands in Arctic Greenland. Ancient peoples made windows by stretching a dried seal bladder over a hole in the wall. The bladder was thin enough to allow light through.

A tent covered with several layers of animal skins made an extremely warm Arctic home, even in the bitterly cold winter. The wooden poles were lashed together with rope.

Lean the five extra bamboo sticks against main frame, placing ends around the base cle. Leave a gap at the nt for the entrance.

5 Tie the middle of the edge of the two larger blankets to the back of the frame, at the top. Make two tight knots to secure the blankets.

6 Bring each blanket round to the entrance. Tie them at the top with string. Roll the blankets down to the base so they lie flat on the frame.

7 Tie five one-metre lengths of thread along the front edge of the blanket. Pull these tight and tie to a log or stone to weigh down the base of the tent.

Seasonal Camps

CHEERFUL GLOW
An igloo near Thule in Greenland is lit up by the glow of a primus stove. The light inside reveals the spiralling shape of the blocks of ice used to make the igloo. Snow crystals in the walls scatter the light so the whole room is bathed in the glow. In the Inuit language, *iglu* was actually a word to describe any type of house. A shelter such as this one was called an *igluigaq*.

SUMMER is a busy time for Arctic animals and plants. The rising temperature melts the sea ice, and the oceans teem with tiny organisms called plankton. On land, the tundra bursts into flower. Insects hatch out and burrowing creatures, such as lemmings, leave their tunnels in search of food. Wild reindeer, whales and many types of birds migrat to the Arctic to feast on the plentiful supply of food.

The lives of Arctic peoples changed with the seasons too. In Canada, Alaska and Greenland, the Inuit left their winte villages and travelled to the summer hunting grounds. They hunted fish and sea mammals and gathered fruits and berries, taking advantage of the long, bright summer days.

During winter hunting trips, the Inuit built temporary shelters made of snow blocks, commonly called igloos. The basic igloo design was developed hundreds of years ago. It ke the hunters warm even in the harshest Arctic storm.

BUILDING AN IGLOO
An Inuk builds an igloo, using a long ice knife to cut large blocks of tightly packed snow. First, he lays a ring of ice bloc to make a circle up to 3 metres in diameter. Then, some of th blocks are cut to make them slope. As new blocks are added, the walls of the igloo begin to lean inwards, forming the familiar dome-shaped igloo. This method is exactly the same as the one used by his ancestors centuries ago.

MAKE A MODEL IGLOO
You will need: self-drying clay, rolling pin, cutting board, ruler, modelling tool, scissors, thick card (20 x 20 cm), pencil, water bowl, white paint, paint brush.

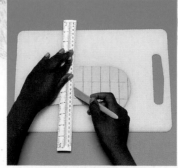

1 Roll out the self-drying clay. It should be around 8 mm thick. Cut out 30 blocks of clay; 24 must be 2 x 4 cm and the other 6 blocks must be 1 x 2 cm.

2 Cut out some card to make an irregular shape. Roll out more clay (8 mm thick). Put the template on the clay and cut around it to make the base of the igloo.

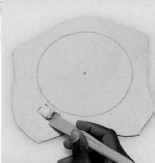

3 Mark out a circle wit a diameter of 12 cm. Cut out a small rectangl on the edge of the circle (2 x 4 cm) to make the entrance to the igloo.

IGLOO VILLAGE

This engraving, made in 1871, shows a large Inuit village in the Canadian Arctic. Most Inuit igloos were simple, dome-like structures. The Inuit built these temporary shelters during the winter hunting trips.

A SNUG HOME

An Inuit hunter shelters inside his igloo. A small entrance tunnel prevents cold winds from entering the shelter and traps warm air inside. Outside, the temperature may be as low as −70°C. Inside, heat from the stove, candles and the warmth of the hunter's body keeps the air at around 5°C.

THE FINAL BLOCK

An Inuit hunter carefully places the final block of ice onto the roof of his igloo. Ancient hunters used sharp ice knives to shape the blocks so that they fitted together exactly. Any gaps were sealed with snow to prevent the icy winds from entering the shelter.

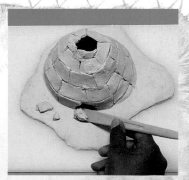

Inuit hunters built temporary shelters by fitting ice blocks together to form a spiralling dome structure called an igloo. Only firmly packed snow was used to make the building blocks.

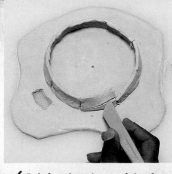

4 Stick nine large blocks around the edge of the circle. Use water to make the clay stick to the base. Cut across two rectangular blocks as shown above.

5 Using your modelling tool, carefully cut a small piece of clay from the corner of each of the remaining blocks as shown above.

6 Starting from the two blocks cut earlier, build up the walls, slanting each block in as you go. Use the six small blocks at the top. Leave a hole at the top.

7 Use the modelling tool to form a small entrance to the igloo behind the rectangle already cut into the base. When the clay has dried, paint the igloo white.

Home Comforts

INSIDE ARCTIC SHELTERS, small comforts made life more bearable. From the earliest times, the Inuit and other Arctic groups used the frozen ground for sleeping platforms, or made them out of snow. Animal skins were draped across the platforms to make them warm and comfortable. Often, the walls and floor were lined with skins to provide extra insulation from the bitter Arctic winds.

The floor of the ancient Nenet and Saami tents was a meshwork of branches covered with animal skins. In the centre of the tent, flat stones made a safe platform for the fire. Arctic peoples started fires with the heat created by a tool called a bow drill. In Inuit shelters, stone lamps burning seal or whale fat provided heat and lit up the darkness. With lamps or candles burning, the shelters were surprisingly warm, and many people took off the outer layers of their clothing as they entered.

ROCKING THE CRADLE

A Nenet baby sleeps in its cradle. The cradle is usually suspended from the stout wooden struts that hold up the tent. The struts make a frame sturdy enough to support fairly heavy weights.

INSIDE AN IGLOO

This engraving of the inside of an igloo was made by the European traveller Edward Finden in 1824. Inuit women hung all their possessions from strings, poles and even reindeer antlers to warm them in the dry air higher in the igloo.

MAKE AN OIL LAMP

You will need: self-drying clay, rolling pin, cutting board, ruler, compass, sharp pencil, modelling tool, water bowl, dark grey and light grey paint, small paint brush.

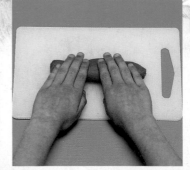

1 Roll out a piece of clay to a thickness of 1 cm. Draw out a circle with a radius of 5 cm, and carefully use the modelling tool to cut the circle out.

2 Using your hands, roll another piece of clay out into a long sausage shape. Make the shape around 30 cm long and 2 cm thick.

3 Wet the edge of the clay circle and stick the sausage shape around it. Use the rounded end of the modelling tool to blend the edges into the base.

FEEDING THE STOVE

A Nenet woman adds another log to the stove to keep her family's reindeer-skin tent warm. She has hung a pair of wet boots above the stove to dry them out. Stoves such as this one were light enough to be carried on sledges pulled by reindeer when it was time to move on.

IN THE FIRELIGHT

A Saami herder warms his hands in the light of a crackling fire inside his tent. You can see a large stack of wood piled up by the fire. Traditionally, the tent floor was a network of birch branches with skins laid over the top. Smoke spiralled upwards and escaped through a hole in the roof.

FIRE AND ICE

Two hunters sit on a skin-covered sleeping platform, keeping warm beside the fire. Most fires were balanced on frames made from driftwood or animal bones. That way, the flames did not go out or melt the floor. Wet clothes and animal skins were often dried on a rack set above the fire.

Stone lamps burning seal or whale blubber (fat) have long cast a warm glow in homes throughout the Arctic. A lighted wick of moss or fur was placed in a bowl filled with the fat and left to burn slowly.

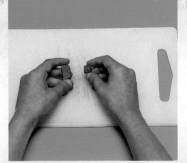

4 Use your modelling tool to cut a small triangular notch at the edge of the circle. This will make a small lip for the front of the lamp.

5 Shape a piece of clay into a small head. Use another piece to shape some shoulders. Stick the head to the shoulders by wetting the clay.

6 Stick the small figure just off the centre of the base of the lamp. Then use the modelling tool to make a small groove on the base to hold the oil.

7 Decorate the edge of the lamp with extra pieces of clay. Once dry, paint the lamp. *Safety note: do not attempt to burn anything in your model lamp.*

Family Life

ARCTIC PEOPLES lived in closely knit families. Most family groups were made up not just of a mother, father and their children, but often grandparents, uncles, aunts and cousins too. These family units often consisted of a dozen people or more, all living in extremely close quarters.

Within the family, men and women had different jobs to do. In Inuit society, men were responsible for hunting. They also maintained the hunting equipment and looked after the dogs that pulled their sledges. Women were responsible for most other chores around the home. Their work included tending the fire, cooking, fetching ice to make drinking water, preparing animal hides and looking after their children. Sewing was another important job for women. They had to find time to make and repair all the family's clothes and bedding. Surviving in the Arctic was hard, and both men and women often worked long hours to keep everyone warm, clothed and fed.

DIVIDING THE WORKLOAD
A Nenet woman pours tea for her husband inside the family tent. In Nenet families, work was divided among members of the family. Traditionally, men herded reindeer. Women did most other tasks. As well as cooking, women pitched and dismantled the tents, chopped wood, prepared animal hides and sewed all the family's clothing.

ALL-PURPOSE KNIFE
This knife, called an *ulu*, was the traditional tool of Inuit women. It was used for many tasks, including cutting meat and preparing animal hides. The *ulu* had a round blade, made from polished slate or metal. The handle was made from bone or wood.

DRAWSTRING PURSE
You will need: shammy leather (21 x 35 cm), PVA glue, glue brush, pencil, ruler, scissors, shoelace (50 cm long), red, dark blue and light blue felt, 2 blue beads.

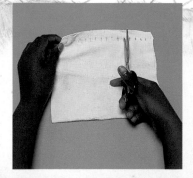

1 Fold over the piece of shammy leather to make a square shape. Glue down two opposite edges, leaving one end open. Let the glue dry.

2 Across the open end of the purse, pencil in marks 1 cm apart on both sides of the leather. Use your scissors to make small holes at these points.

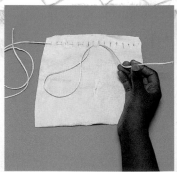

3 Thread a shoelace through the holes on both sides, as shown above. Tie the ends of the shoelace together and leave an excess piece of lace hanging.

CHOPPING ICE

Ice splinters fly as an Inuit hunter chops at a frozen block near a river in the Northwest Territories of Canada. Fetching ice to make drinking water was often a job for women. Once collected, the ice was taken back to the camp and melted over lamps that burned whale or seal blubber (fat).

USING FEATHERS

Arctic women often used the feathers of eider ducks, called eiderdown, to make bedding and warm clothes. Female ducks pluck these feathers from their breasts to help keep their chicks warm in the nest. Women collected the down from the nests or used bird skins complete with feathers. Eiderdown is still used today to make warm quilts.

Eider duck

DRYING SEALSKIN

An Inuit woman stretches a sealskin on a wooden frame to prevent the skin from shrinking as it dries. Preparing animal skins was a woman's job. Using her *ulu,* she would clean the skin by scraping off all the flesh and fat. Then the skin was stretched and dried. Finally, she would soften the hide by chewing it with her front teeth.

FEEDING TIME

An Inuit hunter feeds seal meat to each of his huskies. The Inuits used huskies as draught animals, and they were well looked after by their owners. In winter, they were fed extra meat to provide them with enough energy to pull a heavy sledge in the cold climate.

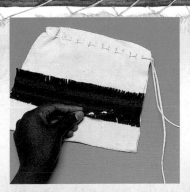

Arctic women often made bags, baskets and other useful containers. Drawstring purses such as this one were made of soft deer hide.

4 Carefully cut two strips of red felt 21 cm long and 5 cm wide. Then, cut a narrow fringe about 1 cm deep along both edges of the felt, as shown above.

5 Glue the strips of red felt to either side of the purse. You can add extra decoration by gluing 1 cm strips of blue felt on other parts of the purse.

6 Tie the two blue beads firmly to each end of the excess shoelace. Close the purse by pulling the shoelace and tying a knot in it.

Arctic Children

MODEL IGLOO

An Inuit toddler plays with a model igloo at a nursery in the Canadian Arctic. The blocks of wood spiral upwards in the same way as the blocks of ice do in a real igloo, so the toy helps modern children to learn the ancient art of building igloos.

CHILDREN were at the centre of most Arctic societies. Inuit babies and younger children spent most of their time riding on their mother's back, nestled in a snug pouch called an *amaut*. The babies of many Arctic groups were named for a respected member of the community and their birth was celebrated with a huge feast. As children grew older, other members of the family helped the mother to bring up her child.

Today, most Arctic children go to school when they are young. However, the children of past generations travelled with their parents as the group moved to fresh reindeer pastures or new hunting grounds. Very young boys and girls were treated equally. As they grew up, however, children helped with different tasks and learned the skills that they would need later on in life. Boys learned how to hunt and look after animals. Girls learned to sew and cook and to work with animal skins.

BIRTHDAY FEAST

Traditional food is prepared at the birthday celebration of the young boy sitting at the table. Parents often named their newborn babies after people who had been respected in the community, such as a great hunter. The baby was thought to inherit that person's skills and personality.

FEEDING BIRDS TOY

You will need: self-drying clay, rolling pin, ruler, modelling tool, board, two toothpicks, white and brown paint, water pot, paint brush.

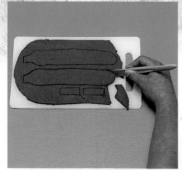

1 Roll out some of the clay into a 22 x 14 cm rectangle with a thickness of around 1 cm. Cut out two large paddles (18 x 3 cm) and two stalks (4 x 2 cm).

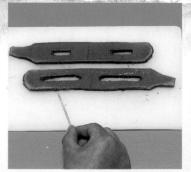

2 Cut two slots on paddle 1 (5 cm x 8 mm) and two on paddle 2 (2.5 cm x 8 mm). Use a toothpick to pierce a hole in the side of paddle 1 through these slots.

3 Roll out two egg shapes, each about 5 x 3.5 cm, in the palm of your hands. Make two bird heads and stick them to the egg-shaped bodies.

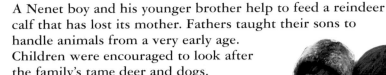

LENDING A HAND

A Nenet boy and his younger brother help to feed a reindeer calf that has lost its mother. Fathers taught their sons to handle animals from a very early age. Children were encouraged to look after the family's tame deer and dogs.

RIDING HIGH

One of the children in this old illustration is being carried in a special hood, called an *amaut,* high on the back of his mother's jacket. The second child is tucked inside her mother's sealskin boots. However, it was less common for a child to be carried in this way.

PLAYING WITH DOLLS

A doll dressed in a soft fleecy coat rests on a Nenet sledge in Arctic Russia. Many Arctic girls like to play with dolls, as children do around the world. Traditionally, the dolls' heads were carved from ivory. The doll in the picture, however, is made of modern plastic.

Some Arctic children had toys with moving parts, such as this model of two birds. Traditionally, the animals would have been carved from bone or ivory. The child pulled the paddles to make the birds bob up and down.

4 Stick the stalks you made earlier to the base of each bird's body. Using the toothpick, pierce a small hole through the stalk, close to the body.

5 Leave the clay bird to dry on its side. You will need to support the stalk with a small piece of clay to hold the bird upright as it dries.

6 Place the stalk of each bird in the slots in the paddles. Push a toothpick into the holes in the edge of paddle 1, through the stalks and out the other side.

7 Add two small pieces of clay to the bottom of each stalk to keep the birds in place. You can paint the toy once the clay has dried.

Fun and Games

THE EARLY YEARS were exciting times for Arctic children, with plenty of time for play and fun. Outdoor games included sliding and sledging on the ice. Indoors, children played traditional games or learned to carve animal bones. In the evenings, everyone gathered round the fire, and adults would tell magical stories featuring brave warriors and terrible monsters. For example, the Saami of Scandinavia told their children tales about *Stallos* – scary monsters that liked to eat people. The hero of the story had to outwit the monster to avoid being eaten.

Ivory, bones, animal hides and sinew (tendons) were all used to make various games and toys. Balls were made from inflated seal bladders. The tiny bones from a seal's flipper were used to make an Inuit version of the game of jacks.

SLEDGING IN THE SNOW
Two children enjoy a toboggan ride in Siberia. Boys and girls who live in the Arctic love to play in the snow. Sledging and playing in the snow help to teach children about the different snow conditions that exist in the region.

GOING HUNTING
An Inuit hunter teaches his son how to read tracks in the snow. Boys learned vital hunting skills from an early age. A boy's first kill was very important and a day he would remember for the rest of his life. To mark the occasion, the boy's parents might hold a feast for all the family to attend. Around the age of twelve, boys were allowed to go on more dangerous hunting trips with their fathers, such as walrus- or whale-hunting expeditions.

HOLE AND PIN GAME
You will need: thin card, ruler, pencil, PVA glue, glue brush, masking tape, scissors, compass, 40 cm length of black thread, thick card, cream paint, paint brush, water pot, chopstick.

1 Using the thin card, mark out a triangle with a base 13 cm long and a height of 15 cm. Roll the triangular piece of card around a pencil to soften it.

2 Shape the softened card into a cone and glue it into position. You may need to secure the cone with a piece of masking tape.

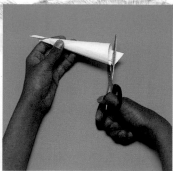

3 Once you have secured it into position, trim off the excess card from the base of the cone. Make sure you always cut away from your body.

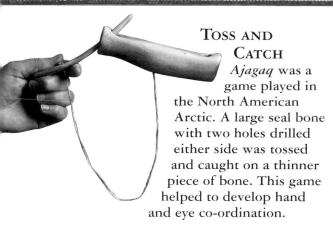

TOSS AND CATCH

Ajagaq was a game played in the North American Arctic. A large seal bone with two holes drilled either side was tossed and caught on a thinner piece of bone. This game helped to develop hand and eye co-ordination.

STRING PUZZLES

An Inuit woman from Greenland shows a traditional puzzle she has made by winding string around her fingers. The shape depicts two musk oxen – large, fearsome Arctic mammals – charging each other. String puzzles were a common way of passing the time during the long Arctic winter. The strings were made from whale sinew (tendons) or long strips of sealskin.

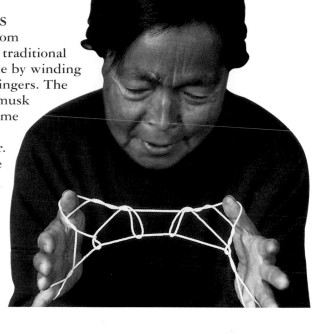

LASSOING GAME

A Chukchi boy from Arctic Russia learns to use a lasso by practising on a reindeer antler. This skill will be essential later on in life. Around the Arctic, various games were played with reindeer antlers. Sometimes children would run around with the antlers on their heads, pretending to be reindeer. The other children would try to lasso or herd them.

Ajagaq was played with two animal bones strapped together with a thin piece of sealskin. Two small holes were drilled at each end of the larger of the two bones. The thinner bone was used to spear the larger bone through one of the holes.

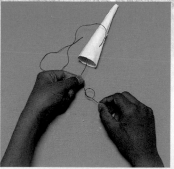

4 Cover the cone in tape. Pierce a hole in the middle of the cone, thread some black thread through, tie a knot on the inside and secure it with tape.

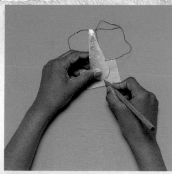

5 Use the base of the cone to draw a circle onto the thicker piece of card. Carefully cut around the circle using your pair of scissors.

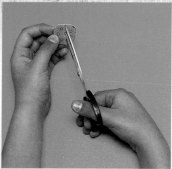

6 Pierce lots of holes through the thick card circle, making sure the chopstick will fit through them. Glue this piece onto the base of the cone.

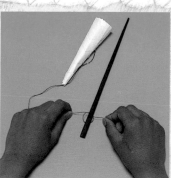

7 Paint the cone carefully, avoiding the holes. Once it has dried, secure the chopstick to the other end of the thread using a tight knot, as shown above.

Over Ice and Snow

DURING THE WINTER, the surface of the Arctic Ocean freezes over and snow covers the land. In the past, sledges were the most common way of travelling over the ice and snow. They were made from bone or timber lashed together with strips of hide or whale sinew. They glided over the snow on runners made from walrus tusks or wood. Arctic sledges had to be light enough to be pulled by animals, yet strong enough to carry an entire family and its belongings. In North America, the Inuit used huskies to pull their sledges. In Siberia and Scandinavia, however, reindeer were used to pull sledges.

In ancient times, Arctic peoples sometimes used skis and snowshoes to get around. Skis are thought to have been invented by the Saami more than 3,500 years ago. Snowshoes allowed Arctic hunters to stalk prey without sinking into deep snowdrifts.

REINDEER SLEDGES
Three reindeer stand by a family and their sledge in Siberia. In Arctic Russia and Scandinavia, reindeer were commonly used to pull sledges. Small, narrow sledges carried just one person. Larger, wider models could take much heavier loads.

HITCHING A DOG TEAM
A husky team struggles up a hill in eastern Greenland. Traditionally, the reins, or traces, used by the dogs to pull the sledge, were made of walrus hide. Different cultures used one of two arrangements to hitch the dogs together. Some people hitched them in the shape of a fan. Others hitched the dogs as pairs in a long line.

MODEL SLEDGE
You will need: thick card, balsa wood, ruler, pencil, scissors, PVA glue, glue brush, masking tape, compass, barbecue stick, string, shammy leather, brown paint, paint brush, water pot.

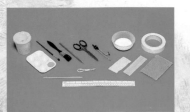

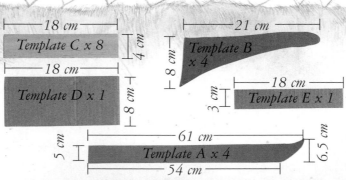

Template C x 8 — 18 cm / 4 cm

Template D x 1 — 18 cm / 8 cm

Template B x 4 — 21 cm / 8 cm

Template E x 1 — 18 cm / 3 cm

Template A x 4 — 61 cm / 54 cm / 5 cm / 6.5 cm

Using the shapes above for reference, measure out the shapes on the card (use balsa wood for template C). Cut the shapes out using your scissors. You will need to make 4 A templates, 4 B templates, 8 C templates (balsa wood), 1 D template and 1 E template. Always remember to cut away from your body when using scissors.

1 Glue 2 A templates together. Repeat this for the other 2 A templates. Repeat this with the 4 B templates. Cover all the edges with masking tape.

SNOWSHOES

Snowshoes are used to walk across deep snowdrifts without sinking into the snow. They spread the person's weight across a large area. To make the snowshoe, thin, flexible birch saplings were steamed to make them supple. The saplings were then bent into the shape of the snowshoe frame. Some shoes were rounded but others were long and narrow. The netting was woven from long strips of animal hide.

birch sapling

snowshoes

rawhide thongs

MAN'S BEST FRIEND

This picture, painted around 1890, shows an Inuit hunter harnessing one of his huskies. Huskies were vital to Inuit society. Out on the hunt, the dogs helped to nose out seals hiding in their dens and hauled heavy loads of meat back to camp.

SAAMI SKIS

The Saami have used skis for thousands of years. The skis were made of wood and the undersides were covered with strips of reindeer skin. The hairs on the skin pointed backwards, allowing the skier to climb up hills.

LET SLEEPING DOGS LIE

A husky's thick coat keeps it warm in temperatures as low as −50°C. These hardy animals can sleep peacefully in the fiercest of blizzards. The snow builds up against their fur and insulates them.

Inuit hunters used wooden sledges pulled by huskies to hunt for food over a large area. The wood was lashed together with animal hide or sinew.

2 Using a compass, make small holes along the top edge of the glued A templates. Use the end of a barbecue stick to make the holes a little larger.

3 Glue the balsa wood slats C in position over the holes along the A templates as shown above. You will need to use all 8 balsa wood slats.

4 Carefully glue the B templates and the E and D templates to the end of the sledge, as shown above. Allow to dry, then paint the model.

5 Thread string through the holes to secure the slats on each side. Decorate the sledge with a shammy-covered card box and secure it to the sledge.

On the Water

I N THE SUMMER, as soon as the sea ice had melted, Arctic people took to the water to hunt. Inuit hunters used one-person canoes called *kayaks* to track their prey. *Kayaks* were powered and steered by a double-bladed paddle. To make the craft more waterproof, the hunter closed up the top of his *kayak,* leaving only a narrow gap to allow him to climb in. The design was so successful that *kayaks* are still in use today.

Kayaks were light, speedy craft, ideal for the solitary hunter to chase seals and small whales. When hunting large bowhead whales, however, Inuit men teamed up into hunting parties of up to ten people and travelled in bigger, open boats called *umiaks.* These craft were also used to transport families across stretches of water and to ferry heavy loads from place to place.

KAYAK TRIP
An engraving made in the 1860s shows an Inuit hunter in a *kayak* chasing a small Arctic whale called a narwhal. The hunter's harpoon is attached to a large float, which is designed to slow down the harpooned whale and prevent its body from sinking when it dies. The hunter's equipment is securely lashed to the *kayak* using thick straps of animal hide.

BUILDING A KAYAK
An Inuit craftsman shapes the final pieces of his *kayak* frame. Traditionally, the wooden frame was covered with sealskins that were sewn together with skilful waterproof seams. All the joints were shaped to fit together exactly or secured with wooden pegs or leather strips.

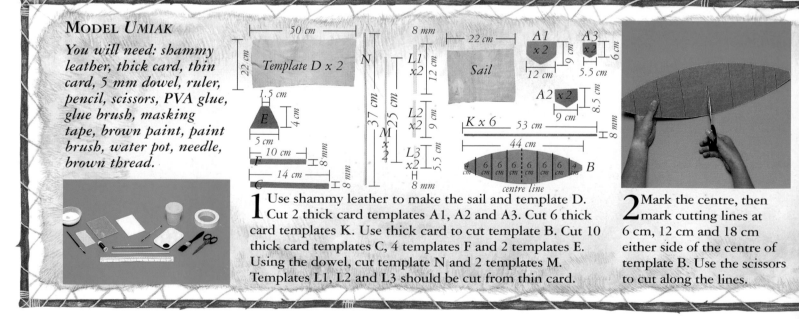

MODEL UMIAK

You will need: shammy leather, thick card, thin card, 5 mm dowel, ruler, pencil, scissors, PVA glue, glue brush, masking tape, brown paint, paint brush, water pot, needle, brown thread.

Template D x 2 — 50 cm — 22 cm
N — 8 mm
L1 x2 — 12 cm
Sail — 22 cm
A1 x 2 — 12 cm — 9 cm
A3 x2 — 5.5 cm — 6 cm
E — 1.5 cm — 4 cm — 5 cm
F — 10 cm — 8 mm
G — 14 cm — 8 mm
M x 2 — 37 cm — 25 cm
L2 x2 — 9 cm
A2 x 2 — 9 cm — 8.5 cm
K x 6 — 53 cm — 44 cm — 8 mm
L3 x2 — 5.5 cm
H — 8 mm
B — 4 cm 6 cm 6 cm 6 cm 6 cm 6 cm 6 cm 4 cm
centre line

1 Use shammy leather to make the sail and template D. Cut 2 thick card templates A1, A2 and A3. Cut 6 thick card templates K. Use thick card to cut template B. Cut 10 thick card templates C, 4 templates F and 2 templates E. Using the dowel, cut template N and 2 templates M. Templates L1, L2 and L3 should be cut from thin card.

2 Mark the centre, then mark cutting lines at 6 cm, 12 cm and 18 cm either side of the centre of template B. Use the scissors to cut along the lines.

UPTURNED *UMIAK*

A photograph taken in Alaska around 1900 shows an Inuit family sheltering inside an upturned *umiak*. *Umiaks* were made of seal or walrus skins stretched over a sturdy wooden or bone frame. They were used to transport large hunting parties or heavy loads.

KAYAK PADDLE

An Inuit hunter shapes a new paddle from a wooden plank. Traditional *kayak* paddles were double-bladed, which made it easier to keep the boat steady in rough seas. The twin blades also allowed the hunters to move through the water more quickly as they pursued their prey.

TREACHEROUS WATERS

A large iceberg drifts in the sea off the coast of Greenland. Arctic waters held many dangers for Inuit hunters. Icebergs were a particular problem when they broke up or rolled. In summer, melting ice at the water's edge made it difficult to get in and out of boats. If a hunter slipped and fell into the icy water, he would last only minutes before dying of exposure.

TRAVEL BY *UMIAK*

Three Inuit hunters paddle a small *umiak* though the icy waters off the coast of Alaska. *Umiaks* were more stable than *kayaks* in rough seas and when hunting larger sea mammals. However, they were much heavier to haul over the ice to the water's edge.

3 Glue the middle section of A onto the sections of template B, as shown above. Use the smallest A templates at the end. Use the largest A template at the centre.

4 Glue 2 strips of template K to both sides of the structure, as shown above. Glue the K templates together at each end of the structure.

5 Weave templates C through templates K and over templates A, as shown. Fix with glue. Leave 1.5 cm excess card at the top of the boat.

6 Stick the ends of C together with masking tape. Repeat the last two stages with F for the smaller ends of the structure.

Continued on next page...

Tools and Weapons

ARCTIC HUNTERS used many different weapons, hand-crafted from materials such as animal hide, bone and ivory. Weapons were kept in the best possible condition, and the hunter would inspect his weapons carefully before setting off each day.

Traditional Arctic weapons included bows and arrows and slingshots, used to bring down game birds, reindeer and other prey. Long three-pronged spears, called *kakivaks,* were used to catch fish. Seals, whales and other sea creatures were hunted with harpoons. Many weapons had barbed tips that lodged in the wounded animal's flesh. Other hunting tools included nets, fish hooks and sun goggles. When hunting in *kayaks,* western Inuits of Alaska or Asia, called Yupiks, wore wooden helmets to protect their eyes from the glare of the sun.

BOW AND ARROW
A Nenet boy hunts birds using a bow and arrow. Bows were made of bone or wood, with a string of twisted sinew. The arrow tips were made from ivory or copper.

SNOW GOGGLES
These Inuit snow goggles are made from the antlers of a reindeer. The hunter peered through the narrow slits. Snow goggles protected hunters' eyes from the reflection of the Sun on the snow, which could cause temporary "snow blindness".

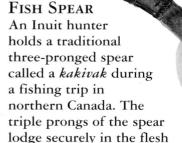

FISH SPEAR
An Inuit hunter holds a traditional three-pronged spear called a *kakivak* during a fishing trip in northern Canada. The triple prongs of the spear lodge securely in the flesh of the fish so that it cannot wriggle free and swim away.

7 Glue the remaining K templates to the sides and ends of the structure as before. Pierce a hole for the mast in the middle of the base of the boat.

8 Glue in templates E to both ends of the structure, as shown above. Now paint the inside of the boat and leave it to dry.

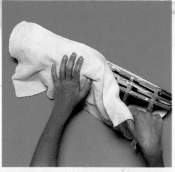

9 Cover the sides of the boat with the shammy leather templates D. Stretch and glue the leather into position, as shown above. Leave the base hanging free.

10 Cut two small slits in the base of templates D. Overlap and curve the leather templates around the base of the structure, as shown above.

HARPOON MAKING

Harpoons were versatile weapons, used to hunt seals, whales and walruses. Each weapon was carefully crafted. Wood and ivory were fitted together to form the shaft and the ivory point was tipped with metal such as copper. The head detached from the shaft on impact. It was securely fastened to a long hide line, in turn the line was attached to a float made of wood or an inflated seal bladder. Today, hunters use a nylon line attached to a float made from an inner tube.

copper

harpoon head

HARPOON AT THE READY

A harpoon rests in the prow of a boat off the coast of Alaska. The harpoon is attached to a float with a length of rope. This makes sure the weapon will not sink and can be retrieved if the hunter misses his target.

HANDY PICK

This Inuit pick is made of a walrus tusk bound to a wooden handle with thin strips of animal hide. Picks such as this one would have been used to hack away at frozen soil or to smash through thick blocks of ice.

Umiaks were large open boats that were around 9 metres (30 feet) long. They carried up to ten people and were powered by oars or a sail. Umiaks were used for transport or for hunting. Women sometimes helped to row the boats.

BIRD NET

An Arctic hunter checks his net, called a *lpu*, for damage. In summer, these nets were used to catch birds known as little auks.

11 Glue the base of templates D into position, as shown above. Stretch the ends of the shammy leather tight to make a neat join.

12 Glue the balsa mast templates M 2 cm and 17 cm down from the top of template N, as shown above. Secure all the pieces with thread.

13 Paint the mast and leave it to dry. Then, carefully stitch the sail to the mast using large overhead stitches, as shown above.

14 Glue and tape the sail into position using the hole you made before. Glue templates L over section pieces A to make seats, and then paint them.

Going Hunting

GOOD FISHING
An Inuk from eastern Greenland sits on his sledge, fishing for halibut through a hole in the ice. He has already caught four fish. Arctic hunters used hooks, nets and spears to catch their prey. In summer, fish were usually taken from lakes or from their river spawning grounds.

ARCTIC PEOPLE were skilled hunters. For most of the year, their diet consisted only of meat. In Russia and Scandinavia, the Saami and other herding peoples ate reindeer meat. In North America and Greenland, the Inuit's main source of food was seals. (In fact, the Inuit word for seal means "giver of life".) Many land animals, such as Arctic hares, musk oxen and nesting birds, were also eaten. Out on the ice or in the water, hunters chased polar bears, fish, walruses and whales.

Only the men went hunting. During the summer, hunters in boats stalked seals and walruses in the water. When the sea froze over in winter, the same creatures were hunted on foot. Arctic hunters worked all year round to provide their families with enough food, even during the long, dark winter days when the Sun never rose in the sky.

STALKING SEALS
A drawing from the 1820s shows two Inuit waiting at seals' breathing holes. In summer, seals climb up onto the ice to sleep in the sunlight. Inuit hunters stalked these seals on foot. If the seal awoke, the hunter would lie on the ice, pretending to be another seal. The best hunters could crawl right up to a seal, grab it by the flipper and club it to death.

HUNTING BLIND
You will need: dark green felt (90 x 65 cm), scissors, ruler, string, 6 bamboo sticks (two 80 cm long and four 55 cm long), masking tape, PVA glue, glue brush, light green felt, pencil, leaves.

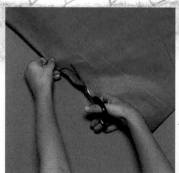

1 Fold the dark green felt in half along its length. Using your scissors, cut a small hole in the centre of the felt on the fold, as shown above.

2 Tie a length of string to one end of two 55 cm lengths of bamboo. Use tape to hold the string in position, leaving a 10 cm length of string hanging.

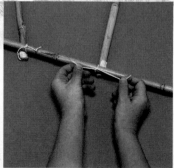

3 Tie the ends of these two 55 cm long bamboo poles to the area around the middle of one of the 80 cm lengths of bamboo, as shown above.

UNDER COVER

Today, modern Inuit hunters use rifles for hunting prey. The Inuk pictured above is also using a screen called a hunting blind to stalk a seal. The hunting blind conceals the hunter from the watchful eyes of seals. Both the screen and rifle are mounted on a small sledge, which allows the hunter to advance slowly towards his target.

IN FOR THE KILL

This engraving shows an Inuit hunter aiming his harpoon at a seal that has come to the surface of the water to breathe. Silent and motionless, hunters would wait at these breathing holes for hours if necessary. The tiniest noise or vibration at the surface would frighten the animal away. When the seal finally surfaced, the hunter would spear it and drag it from the hole. The hunter would then kill the seal by clubbing it over the head.

NETTING BIRDS

An Inuk nets a little auk on the rocky slopes of Pitufik in northwest Greenland. In spring, millions of birds migrate to the Arctic to lay eggs and rear their young. The Inuit and other groups caught these birds by using nets or by throwing weighted strings, known as *bolas*, at the birds.

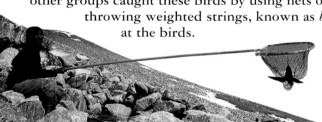

The Inuit and other Arctic peoples used hunting blinds to sneak up on prey, such as seals. Most hunting blinds were white so they blended in with the snow. A green blind would work better in a leafy landscape.

4 Glue the other 55 cm bamboo poles to the two shorter edges of the felt. Glue the last 80 cm pole to one of the longer edges. Tape the bamboo at the corners.

5 Glue the 80 cm bamboo pole from stage three to the fourth edge of the felt. Make sure to glue around the lengths of bamboo that are tied on.

6 Draw some leaf shapes on the light green felt, and use your scissors to cut the shapes out. Always cut away from your body when using scissors.

7 Decorate the hunting blind by sticking the leaves to the front of the screen. You can glue some real leaves to the hunting blind for more effect.

Big Game Hunters

As WELL AS SMALLER PREY, such as seals and fish, Arctic people also hunted large and dangerous creatures, such as musk oxen, whales and polar bears. Hunting these animals was a risky business. A huge whale could easily swamp and capsize an *umiak*. Stranded in the icy water, the hunters would die of exposure in a matter of minutes. A cornered polar bear was an equally dangerous creature. One swipe of its enormous paws was enough to kill any hunter. This fierce predator is also one of the few animals in the world that hunts humans.

Musk oxen were also well able to defend themselves. These large, hairy mammals had long, sharp horns that could impale an unfortunate hunter, inflicting a fatal wound. Hunting dangerous beasts such as these required a team of men and careful planning. If the hunters were successful, one kill could provide enough meat to feed their families for many days.

FEROCIOUS HUNTER
A polar bear stands over a seal it has caught in Arctic Norway. The polar bear is a fearsome creature, with its mighty claws and razor-sharp teeth. This did not deter Inuit hunters, however. They would set their dogs on a bear to keep it at bay, and spear it when they got close enough.

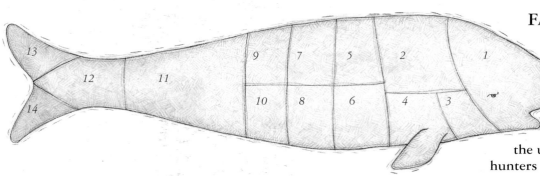

FAIR SHARES
When a white whale was killed, the animal was divided between the hunters so that everyone had a share of the meat. Whales were split up in a particular way. The man who threw the first harpoon got the whale's head and part of the underside (shares 1, 2, 3 and 10). Other hunters and the boat owner got other shares.

SNOW GOGGLES

You will need: a piece of thin card, ruler, pencil, scissors, shammy leather (22 x 6 cm), black pen, PVA glue, glue brush, compass, elastic.

20 cm
1 cm
4 cm
Eyeholes
6 cm
4 mm

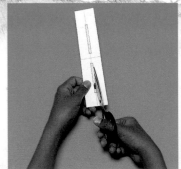

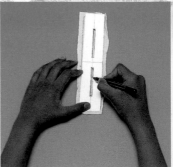

1 Cut the piece of card to 20 x 4 cm. Find the centre of the piece of card, and mark eyeholes 1 cm from the centre. The holes should be 6 cm x 4 mm.

2 Carefully cut out the eyeholes using the ends of your scissors to pierce the card. Always cut away from your body when using scissors.

3 Place the card onto the piece of shammy leather. Use the card as a template and draw around the goggles shape. Remember to draw in the eyeholes.

A USEFUL CREATURE

Whales were valuable Arctic animals. Every part of a whale's body was used. The flesh, fat and internal organs were divided between all the hunters. Some of the meat was given to the dogs. The whale's skin, called *muktuk,* was eaten as a delicacy. The blubber was burned in lamps to provide light and heat. Finally, the huge bones were used to build shelters or carved into weapons and tools.

muktuk

whalebone

MUSK OX CIRCLE

A circle of musk oxen surround their young to protect them against predators. Musk oxen are peaceful tundra animals unless threatened. Then, the adults lower their heads and ward off attackers with their curving horns. Arctic hunters were wary of musk oxen but still hunted them for food.

WHALE HUNT

Teams of Inuit hunters used *umiaks* to hunt large whales, such as bowheads. The oarsmen kept the boat steady so that skilled marksmen could launch their harpoons at the whale. A wounded whale would attempt to dive or swim away, but floats attached to the harpoons would pull the whale back to the surface. Gradually, the animal would become exhausted. Finally, hunters lanced the animal to death and hauled it to the shore.

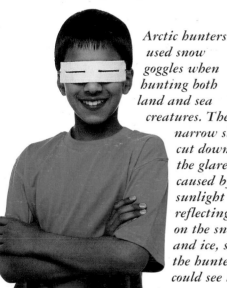

Arctic hunters used snow goggles when hunting both land and sea creatures. The narrow slits cut down the glare caused by sunlight reflecting on the snow and ice, so the hunter could see his prey more clearly.

4 Cut round the goggles shape, leaving a small trim around the edge. Cut down the centre of the eyeholes you have drawn on the shammy leather.

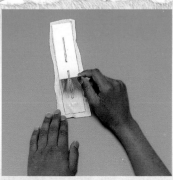

5 Glue the card onto the shammy leather, making sure that you carefully match up the eyeholes on the leather and the card.

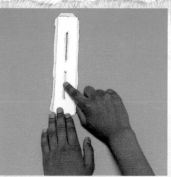

6 Fold back the leather trim and glue it to the back of the card. Open up the eyeholes, fold those edges back and glue them to the card.

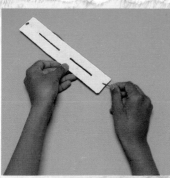

7 Pierce a small hole at either end of the goggles and thread elastic through the holes. Tie a knot at the end. Make sure the elastic fits around your head.

Hunting Magic

Arctic societies had a great respect for nature and the animals they hunted. They believed that all creatures, like people, had spirits. When they killed an animal, they performed rituals that helped to appease (calm) the creature's spirit. The Inuit, for example, beheaded a slain beast to help the animal's spirit leave its body. They made offerings of food and drink in the hope that the animal's spirit would be reborn to be hunted again. Other Arctic hunters put parts of creatures they had killed back into the sea. Hunters took only what they needed to survive. They wasted nothing.

Arctic groups had many taboos, which were rules linked with spiritual practices. Hunting, in particular, was surrounded by many taboos. If a hunter broke a taboo, his action would anger the spirits and he might never hunt successfully again. Shamans were respected members of the community who talked to spirits. They provided a link between ordinary Arctic people and these powerful spirits. Shamans conducted ceremonies to bring good luck to hunting parties.

SACRED PILLAR
Inuksuk, pictured above, are stone columns built by Inuit groups in ancient times. Some are very old. They are linked with hunting taboos and some have a religious meaning. The pillars were built to resemble a person with his or her arms outstretched. (The Inuit word *inuksuk* means "like a person".) They marked routes and channelled migrating reindeer into places where hunters could ambush and kill them.

A RESPECTED BEAST
This ivory carving of a polar bear comes from Greenland. Many taboos surrounded the hunting of these highly respected creatures. The Inuit held polar bears in high esteem because they were thought to look and act in the same way as humans, particularly when they reared up on their hind legs.

WHALE BOX
This wooden box is carved in the shape of a whale. It held the lance points used to harpoon whales. The Inuit and other Arctic groups believed that prey animals, such as whales, were more likely to accept being killed by weapons carved in their image. The lance points would also experience being inside a "whale" and would therefore be more likely to hit their target.

MAGIC SCRATCHER

This "Nunivak tusk" was made as a souvenir in the 1920s. When hunting seals, the Inuit sometimes made screeching noises by scraping ivory scratchers such as this one over the ice. The noise attracted seals to within striking distance of their harpoons. Scratchers were often carved into the shape of the seal's head. Arctic hunters thought this would bring them good luck in future hunting trips.

SPRING CEREMONY

The Chukchi people offer sea spirits food at the edge of the water. The Chukchi took to the seashore early in the spring. They offered food to appease the spirits of the sea. This ritual helped to ensure that the year's hunting would be successful. Elsewhere, when a mighty whale was killed, the hunters held a festival to thank the sea spirits for their generosity.

SYMPATHETIC MAGIC

Drag handles were tools that helped hunters haul animals over the ice after they had been killed. The one shown here is decorated with the heads of three polar bears. Hunters' weapons were often carved to resemble the animals they hunted. This was sympathetic magic, which would help to appease the animal's spirit and bring the hunter good luck in future hunting expeditions.

Food and Feasts

FOR MOST OF THE YEAR, Arctic people lived on a diet of fish and game known as "land food". The fat, flesh, organs and skin of seals, whales, reindeer and other animals contained all the proteins, minerals and vitamins needed for a healthy diet. Vegetables and grain crops, such as wheat, were difficult to grow in most parts of the Arctic region. Few plants could thrive in the frozen soil.

In winter, food was scarce and animals were the main source of food. In the summer, however, food was more varied. People feasted on berries, hunted seabirds and gathered eggs. Siberian and Saami women collected fungi that grew taller than Arctic plants, which were smaller. In autumn, when the reindeer were slaughtered, a great feast was held. Everyone kept very busy, gathering and storing food for the winter months ahead.

EATING RAW MEAT
A Nenet boy from the Yamal Penisula of western Siberia feasts on raw reindeer meat. Arctic people often ate their meat raw. Cooking used up scarce fuel and destroyed some of the valuable vitamins the meat contained.

DRYING MEAT
An Inuit hunter from northwest Greenland lays strips of narwhal meat on the rocks to dry them. Drying meat in this way was an excellent way of preserving food in the summer. The intestines were washed clean and also dried in this way. Meat was also hidden under the rocks to prevent foxes, wolverines and other carnivorous animals from stealing it. If the meat was left for many months, it developed a strong smell and flavour, but it was unlikely to make anyone ill. In winter, the icy temperatures prevented meat from going off, so preserving food was not a problem. The bodies of slain animals could be buried under rocks in the snow near the house and dug up when needed.

FILLETS OF FISH
Inuit hunters arrive back at the shore with a catch of fish known as char. Traditionally, women cleaned and filleted the fish, then hung them up on racks to dry and preserve them. They scored the fishes' flesh into squares to speed up the drying process.

BERRIES
Many types of berries grow wild on the Arctic tundra. They include bilberries, cranberries and cloudberries. Ripe berries contain valuable vitamins. Autumn was the time for picking berries, when they were eaten fresh, and could also be frozen.

bilberries   *cranberries*   *cloudberries*

BIRD'S EGGS

This picture shows three eggs in an eider duck's nest. In the spring, many nesting birds came to the Arctic to rear their young. Their eggs were a valuable source of food and protein for Arctic people and helped to vary the basic diet of meat.

TASTY MEAL
A Nenet woman cooks a meal for her family. In all Arctic societies it was the woman who did the cooking, making meat stews and other traditional dishes. Children often clustered around the fire to steal a taste from the pot.

SAAMI FARMERS
A Saami reindeer herder erects a tent by his summer pastures. In Scandinavia, the Saami are able to farm along the shores of narrow coastal inlets called fjords. On these jagged coasts the land is sheltered from icy winds, so cattle and sheep can graze. Some meadows are mown to make hay to feed the animals in winter.

The Coming of Europeans

ARCTIC ATTACKERS
This early illustration shows a group of Inuit in conflict with English explorers led by a sea captain named Martin Frobisher. Frobisher led one of the first expeditions to Baffin Island in northeast Canada, where his sailors met with strong opposition from the local people.

VIKING RAIDERS
This early drawing shows Viking warriors attacking an Inuit settlement in Greenland. Vikings were the first Europeans to reach the Arctic. In AD983, a group of Vikings led by Erik the Red established two colonies on Greenland. These Viking settlements survived until about 1500.

BEFORE 1600, only a tiny handful of Europeans had ever visited the Arctic. After this time, however, travellers began to arrive in larger numbers. Explorers from Britain, France, Holland and Russia searched for a short cut to China and the Pacific Ocean through the seas north of Canada and Siberia. The sea route north of Canada was known as the Northwest Passage; the route north of Siberia was called the Northeast Passage. From the late 1500s, the British explored the northern coast of Canada. In the 1700s, the Russians mapped Siberia and travelled to Alaska, crossing a sea we now call the Bering Strait.

In the end, European explorers failed to find clear sea routes to the Pacific through the ice-laden waters of the Arctic Ocean. However, they did return with tales of waters teeming with whales and other sea creatures. Whaling ships and other hunters soon followed. Every spring, European ships would cross the northern Atlantic Ocean to slaughter whales. Arctic whale oil was used as a source of fuel for European lamps. These giant creatures were also killed for their valuable "whalebone", or baleen.

ROSS EXPEDITION

This picture shows British explorers John Ross and William Parry meeting with the Inuit of northwest Greenland in August 1818. A powerful female shaman had predicted the arrival of strange men in huge boats with "white wings" – actually sailing ships.

WHALE PRODUCTS

European countries found many uses for the whales they killed. Oil from whale blubber was burned to provide light and heat and also made into soap. Whale oil was used in many foods, including ice cream and margarine. Tough, springy baleen was made into many different products, including brushes, umbrellas, corsets and fishing rods.

soap

margarine

LEARNING FROM THE ARCTIC PEOPLES

In 1909, US explorer Robert Peary became the first man to reach the North Pole, helped by teams of Inuit. Peary wore snowshoes and Inuit-style clothing and used huskies to pull sledges in the same way as the Inuit. Many early European explorers died in the Arctic because they did not use the survival techniques developed by Arctic dwellers. Later expeditions drew on local peoples' experience and were more successful.

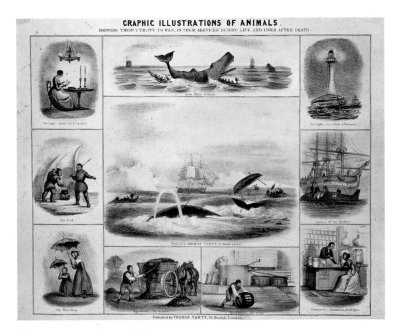

WHALEBONE CORSET

This picture is taken from a catalogue dating back to the early 1900s. It shows a woman wearing a fashionable corset. Women wore these tight undergarments to keep their figures in shape. Corsets were strengthened with bony plates called baleen, which came from the mouths of whales. Baleen was also known as whalebone.

HUNTING THE WHALE

The illustration in the centre of this picture shows an early European whale hunt. Small open hunting boats were launched from a larger ship. Around the main picture, some of the ways in which the whales were used are shown. Europeans saw the whale as an extremely valuable resource.

Cold-weather Clothing

IN THE BITTERLY COLD WINDS and snowstorms, Arctic people needed warm, waterproof clothing to survive. They used animal skins to insulate them from the harsh conditions. Two layers of skins were worn – a tough outer layer with the fur facing outwards and soft, warm underclothes with the fur facing inwards. The fur of the underclothes trapped a layer of warm air next to the person's skin, thus maintaining a constant body temperature. Only a tiny part of a person's body was left exposed to the freezing air.

Outer garments included hooded coats made from reindeer skin, trousers made from the hide of polar bears, and deer- or sealskin boots. When hunting in *kayaks,* Inuit men often wore waterproof *anoraks* (an Inuit word) made from thin strips of seal intestine sewn together. Underclothes included seabird-skin vests and socks made from the skins of reindeer calves.

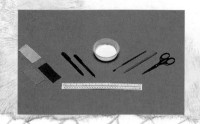

FUR COAT
This girl is wearing a *yagushka,* the traditional jacket worn by Nenet women. The girl's mother has used dark strips of reindeer skin to decorate the jacket. Mittens and a fur-trimmed hood provide extra protection against the icy winds.

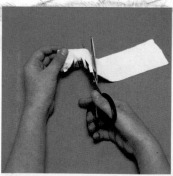

GRASS-LINED BOOTS
A Saami herder lines his reindeer-skin boots with dried grass. Hay provided a soft padding and also trapped a layer of air inside the boots to protect the herder's feet against the bitter cold.

MAKE SOME MITTENS
You will need: 4 pieces of shammy leather, black marker, scissors, PVA glue, glue brush, ruler, light blue and red felt, black pen.

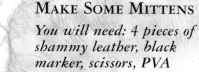

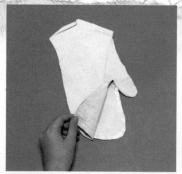

1 Draw around your hand on a piece of shammy leather, leaving a 1.5 cm gap around your hand shape. You will need two pieces of leather per hand.

2 Glue around the edge of the right-hand glove and glue a left-hand glove into position. Repeat this with the other two glove shapes. Leave them to dry.

3 Cut out two pieces of shammy leather, each approximately 20 x 5 cm. Cut a 2 cm fringe on the edge of each piece of shammy leather.

PREPARING SKINS

This Inuit woman is chewing a piece of sealskin to soften it. She uses her front teeth so the skin does not get too wet. In the past, the teeth of old women were worn right down by years of chewing skins. The skin of a bearded seal was used to make the soles of sealskin boots, because it was waterproof and gripped the ice well.

SEWING MATERIALS

Arctic women made all their family's clothes by hand. Bone or antler needles were shaved to a fine point, then rubbed smooth on stones so they did not snag or tear the animal skins. Whale or reindeer sinew was used as thread. When wet, the sinew swelled slightly to make the seams waterproof. Today, Arctic women sew with fine steel needles and use dental floss as thread. Cotton wool is now used to line boots instead of grass.

cotton wool

dental floss

grasses

DRESSED IN SKINS

Inuit hunters wore warm jackets, such as this parka, as well as leggings made from reindeer hide and *kamik*, or sealskin, boots. The warm hood of the jacket helped to preserve body heat. Hoods were often trimmed with wolf or wolverine hair, because these furs shed the ice that formed as the person breathed.

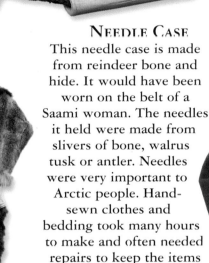

NEEDLE CASE

This needle case is made from reindeer bone and hide. It would have been worn on the belt of a Saami woman. The needles it held were made from slivers of bone, walrus tusk or antler. Needles were very important to Arctic people. Hand-sewn clothes and bedding took many hours to make and often needed repairs to keep the items warm and waterproof.

Rather than gloves, people of the Arctic wore fingerless mittens to keep their hands warm. Children's mittens were sometimes sewn into the sleeves of their parka to stop them from getting lost. Some mittens were embroidered with decorative patterns.

4 Glue along the edge of the fringe shammy and position it around the wrist area of one of the mittens. Make sure the fringe faces forwards.

5 Use a black marker to draw six blue flower shapes (about 5 cm in diameter) and six red circles (about 8 mm in diameter). Cut these shapes out.

6 Glue the red dots you have made to the centre of each blue flower. Repeat this procedure for all six blue flowers and wait for the glue to dry.

7 Decorate the back of the mittens with the flowers. Cut two flowers in half for the wrists and draw in the leaves and stalks with a black pen.

Costumes and Ornaments

ARCTIC CLOTHES were often beautiful as well as practical. Strips or patches of different furs were used to form designs and geometric patterns on outer clothes. Fur trimmings, toggles and other decorative fastenings added the final touches to many clothes. Jewellery included pendants, bracelets, necklaces and brooches. These ornaments were traditionally made of natural materials, such as bone and walrus ivory.

In North America, Inuit women often decorated clothes with birds' beaks, tiny feathers or even porcupine quills. In Greenland, lace and glass beads were popular decorations. Saami clothes were the most colourful in the Arctic. Saami men, women and children wore blue outfits with a bright red and yellow trim. Men's costumes included a tall hat and a short flared tunic. Women's clothes included flared skirts with embroidered hems and colourful hats, shawls and scarves.

SAAMI COSTUME

A Saami man wears the traditional costume of his region, including a flared tunic trimmed with bright woven ribbon at the neck, shoulders, cuffs and hem. Outfits such as the one above were worn all year round. In winter, Saami people wore thick fur parkas, called *peskes,* over the bright tunics.

BEAR TOGGLE

An ivory toggle carved into the shape of a polar bear completes this traditional sealskin jacket. Arctic people took great pride in their appearance and loved to decorate their clothes in this way. In ancient times, the Inuit, for example, decorated their garments with hundreds of tiny feathers or the claws of mammals, such as foxes or hares. Women often decorated all the family's clothes.

MAKE A SAAMI HAT

You will need: red felt (58 x 30 cm), PVA glue, glue brush, black ribbon (58 x 2 cm), coloured ribbon, white felt, ruler, pencil, compass, red card, scissors, red, green and white ribbon (3 at 44 x 4 cm), red ribbon (58 x 4 cm).

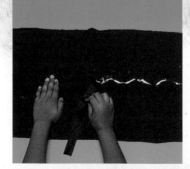

1 Mark out the centre of the red felt along its length. Carefully glue the length of black ribbon along the centre line, as shown above.

2 Continue to decorate the felt with different kinds of coloured ribbon and white felt, making a series of strips along the red felt, as shown above.

3 Cut out a circle of red card with a diameter of 18 cm. Draw a circle inside with a diameter of 15 cm. Cut into the larger circle to the 15 cm line.

CURVING BOOT

This picture shows a curved boot worn by the Saami people from Arctic Scandinavia. These boots are designed for use with skis and are decorated with traditional woollen pompoms. The curved boot tips stop the skier from slipping out of the skis when travelling uphill.

WEDDING FINERY

The bride, bridegroom and a guest at a Saami wedding in north Norway all wear the traditional outfits. Notice that the style of the man's wedding hat differs from the one shown in the picture on the opposite page. Both men and women wear brooches encrusted with metal discs. Saami women's wedding outfits include tall hats, tasselled shawls and ribbons.

BEADS AND LACE

A woman from western Greenland wears the traditional beaded costume of her nation, which includes a top with a wide black collar and cuffs and high sealskin boots. After European settlers arrived in Greenland, glass beads and lace became traditional decorations on clothing. Hundreds of beads were sewn onto jackets to make intricate patterns.

The style of Saami hats varied from region to region. In southern Norway, men's hats were tall and rounded. Further north, their hats had four points.

4 Glue the ends of the decorated red felt together, as shown above. You will need to find the right size to fit around your head.

5 Fold down the tabs cut into the red card circle. Glue the tabs, then stick the card circle to the felt inside one end of the hat.

6 While the hat is drying, glue the coloured ribbon strips together. Glue these strips 15 cm from the end of the 58 cm long red ribbon band.

7 Glue the 58 cm band of red ribbon onto the base of the hat, making sure the shorter strips of red, green and white ribbons go over the top of the band.

107

Arts and Crafts

ARCTIC PEOPLE were accomplished artists. Tools, weapons and ornaments were all made by hand. Across the Arctic, men and women were skilled at carving, sewing, leather-work, basket-making, beadwork and, in some areas, metal-working. In ancient times, objects were always made to be as useful as possible and were not seen as works of art. Today, however, tools and ornaments made by Arctic craftspeople are prized as works of art and fetch high prices when they are sold around the world.

Carving was one of the most important arts in the Arctic, but carving materials were always scarce. Artists engraved designs on bone and ivory, and they carved stone, bone, ivory and reindeer antler into tools and sculptures. Carving tools included knives, needles and bow drills. Some carvings were polished using natural abrasives, such as sand, stone and rough animal skin.

FINE CARVING
This Inuit soapstone carving shows a hunter with his harpoon at the ready. Arctic carvings traditionally featured animals and birds of the region, scenes from everyday life and figures from myths and legends. They were made using knives, needles and bow drills.

MALE AND FEMALE ARTISTS
This early photograph, taken in 1900, shows an Inuit hunter using a bow drill to carve a piece of ivory. His wife makes a pair of *mukluks,* or deerskin boots. Today, Inuit sculptors use electrical power tools as well as knives and hand-drills for carving.

INUIT CARVING
You will need: a bar of soap (about 10 x 7 cm), dark coloured felt-tip pen, a metal nail file.

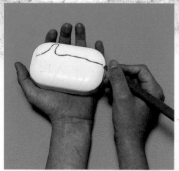

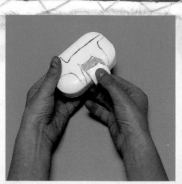

1 First wash your hands so that the bar of soap does not get marked. Draw out the basic shape of a dog on the bar of soap using your felt-tip pen.

2 Begin the carving by cutting away the excess areas of soap around the shape you have drawn. Always make sure you cut away from your hand.

3 Carefully cut away the largest areas of the soap first, as shown above. Make sure the soap does not crumble as you break the pieces away.

SOAPSTONE POTS

Pots and other containers were sometimes made from soapstone (steatite) in the Arctic. This stone is soft enough to carve and hollow out. Knives and bow drills were used as carving tools. People often made long trips by dogsled to collect the stone from the places in which it was found.

soapstone

HAND-CRAFTED TOOLS

This cup and knife were crafted by Saami artists. The cover of the long knife is made from the antler of a reindeer and has been engraved with a decorative pattern. The handle is covered with leather. The drinking cup is carved from a piece of wood. You can just see the small piece of reindeer antler set into the handle of the cup.

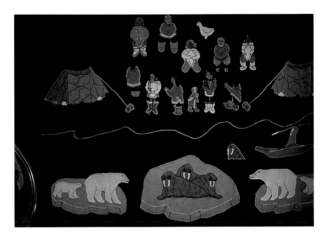

PRINT-MAKING

An artist from Holman Island in the Canadian Arctic works on her print, dabbing paint through a stencil using a short, stubby brush. Print-making is a relatively new craft in the Arctic, but many of the subjects chosen are traditional.

SKILFUL STITCHERS

This picture shows a wall hanging from an Inuit church in Canada. Arctic women were skilled sewers. Many clothes and items such as blankets are now considered works of art.

In the Arctic, carving is a skill that dates back thousands of years. Weapons, tools and various ornaments were carved from natural materials, such as bone, ivory, stone or driftwood.

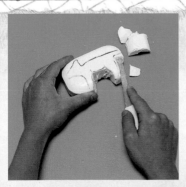

4 Carve away the smaller areas to make the shape more detailed. You should see the basic shape of the dog appear. Continue to carve the soap slowly.

5 Once you have cut out the basic shape of the dog, gradually and gently smooth the rough edges away. The legs and tail will be particularly fragile.

6 Continue to shape the smaller areas to give the dog carving more detail around the ears, legs, tail, stomach, neck and snout.

7 Finally, carefully carve out the smaller features of the head, such as the mouth and the eyes. Flatten the feet so the dog can stand on its legs.

Beliefs and Rituals

Long before Christian missionaries arrived in the Arctic, local people had developed their own beliefs. Arctic people thought that all living creatures possessed a spirit or *inua*. When an animal died, its spirit lived on and was reborn in another creature. Powerful spirits were thought to control the natural world, and these invisible forces influenced people's everyday lives. Some spirits were believed to be friendly towards humans. Others were malevolent or harmful. People showed their respect for the spirits by obeying taboos – rules that surrounded every aspect of life. If a taboo was broken the spirits would be angered. People called shamans could communicate with the spirit world. Shamans had many different roles in the community. They performed rituals to bring good luck in hunting, predicted the weather and the movements of the reindeer herds and helped to heal the sick. They worked as doctors, priests and prophets, all rolled into one.

SHAMAN AND DRUM
An engraving from the early 1800s shows a female shaman from Siberia. Most, but not all, shamans were male. Shamans often sang and beat on special drums, such as the one shown above, to enter a trance. Some drums had symbols drawn on them and helped the shamans to predict the future.

TUPILAK CARVING
This little ivory carving from Greenland shows a monster called a *tupilak. Tupilaks* were evil spirits. If someone wished an enemy harm, he might secretly make a little carving similar to this, which would bring a real *tupilak* to life. It would destroy the enemy unless the person possessed even more powerful magic to ward it off.

SHAMAN'S DRUM
You will need: ruler, scissors, thick card, PVA glue, glue brush, masking tape, compass, pencil, shammy leather, brown paint, paint brush, water pot, brown thread or string

1 Cut out two strips of thick card, each strip measuring 77 cm long and 3 cm wide. Glue the two strips together to give the card extra thickness.

2 Once the glue has dried, use masking tape to cover the edges of the double-thickness card. Try to make the edges as neat as possible.

3 Using a compass, draw a circle with a 24 cm diameter on a piece of shammy leather. Cut it out, leaving a 2 cm strip around the edge of the circle.

HERBAL MEDICINES

An Innu woman collects pitcher plants that she will use to make herbal medicines. In ancient times, shamans acted as community doctors. They made medicines from plants and gave them to sick people to heal them. They also entered trances to soothe angry spirits, which helped the sick to recover from their illness.

SEA SPIRIT

This beautiful Inuit sculpture shows a powerful spirit called Sedna. The Inuit believed that Sedna controlled storms and all sea creatures. If anyone offended Sedna, she withheld her blessing and hunting was poor. Here Sedna is portrayed with a mermaid's tail and accompanied by a narwhal and two seals. This very delicate carving has been made from a piece of reindeer antler.

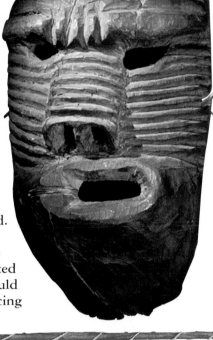

MAGIC MASK

This mask is from Arctic North America. It was worn by Inuit shamans during a special ritual to communicate with the spirit world. Shamans wore wooden masks similar to this one. They also wore head-dresses. Each mask represented a powerful spirit. The shaman would call on the spirit by chanting, dancing and beating on a special drum.

Shamans' drums were made of deerskin stretched over a round wooden frame. The shaman sometimes drew pictures of people, animals and stars on the side of the drum.

4 Using your fingers, curve the strip of card, as shown above. Make sure you curve the card slowly so that it does not crease.

5 Glue the card onto the circle. Ask someone to help keep the shammy leather stretched as you go. Tape the ends of the card together.

6 Make cuts 3 cm apart along the edge of the excess shammy leather towards the card, as shown above. Glue the edges to the cardboard ring.

7 Paint the card with dark brown paint and leave it to dry. Decorate the drum with thick brown thread or string by tying it around the edges.

The Long Polar Night

W INTER LASTS FOR MANY MONTHS IN THE ARCTIC. Communities living in the far north experience nearly three months of darkness in winter, because the Sun never rises above the horizon. During the long, dark days and nights, ancient peoples gathered round the fire to keep warm. The men still went out hunting so their families could eat, but there were many days when bad weather kept them in the camp. During this time, the family came together and listened to stories, sang, laughed and swapped jokes. The older people told myths and legends that had been passed down for generations. These stories explained the existence of the heavens or told how people and animals came to live in the Arctic. Adults practised crafts and taught their children new skills. Men carved tools and fixed their hunting equipment, while women repaired the family's clothes and bedding. Winter was also a time for making ornaments, such as bracelets and brooches. Children practised with string puzzles and played traditional games such as *ajagaq*.

SAAMI SONG
This Saami man is singing a traditional song called a *joik* (pronounced yoik). These light-hearted songs were made up on the spot, and there were no instruments to accompany the singer. These songs told the story of the day's events but used nonsense words and puns. Often, they poked fun at friends and family.

SINGING AND DRUMMING
Four young men perform a traditional drum-song in the Northwest Territories of Canada. Music provided entertainment during long Arctic evenings. Families sang and beat on skin drums with sticks of bone or reindeer antler.

MAKE A BROOCH
You will need: ruler, compass, pencil, thin card, scissors, PVA glue, glue brush, large button, aluminium foil, small roll of sticky tape, small nail varnish bottle, masking tape, safety pin.

1 Using the ruler, set your compass to draw a circle with a diameter of 8 cm on the thin card. Mark the circle lightly in pencil.

2 Cut the 8 cm circle out with your pair of scissors. When using scissors, always make sure that you cut away from your body.

3 Carefully glue the large button to the centre of the card circle. The compass point will have marked out the centre of the circle for you.

MYTHS AND LEGENDS

In the story illustrated to the right, a young Inuit called Taligvak uses magic to catch a seal at a time when other hunters in his village are finding it impossible to catch food. During the long Arctic winter, young children listened to stories like these told by their parents and grandparents. In this way, traditional legends passed down the generations.

The Saami of Lapland used beautiful brooches to fasten their jackets and shawls.

A TIME FOR CRAFTS

Beadwork is a traditional craft in Siberia. The Arctic winter was a good time to practise all kinds of crafts and to repair equipment. Men mended fishing nets and harpoons, while the women stitched new clothes and bedding and repaired garments that had got torn.

4 Cover the front of the card and the button with aluminium foil. Fold the edge over onto the back of the card circle and secure it with glue.

5 Draw around the inside of a small roll of sticky tape on a piece of foil. Repeat this 24 times. Cut out the silver foil circles with your scissors.

6 Place each foil circle over the lid of the nail varnish bottle, and carefully mould the edges over the lid to make 24 small discs.

7 Glue the discs onto the brooch, starting from the middle and working out. Tape a safety pin to the back of the brooch to make a fastening.

Ceremonies and Festivals

ARCTIC CEREMONIES were important occasions. If somebody died, a ceremony was performed to honour that person. In Inuit society, if someone died in an igloo a hole was cut in the wall of the igloo to carry the dead person out. The body was then sewn into a skin bag and laid out on the ground to face the rising Sun. Finally, the body was buried under a mound of stones. The Chukchi of Siberia believed that when a person died, their spirit went to live in the camps of the "Realm of the Polar Star". People were laid to rest with prize possessions that would help them in the afterlife. A great seamstress would be buried with her needles, thread and thimbles. A hunter was buried with his favourite weapons.

People also came together for festivals during the Arctic year. Spring drum ceremonies celebrated the return of the light and the approaching time of plenty. People met to feast, gossip, dance and sing. Other ceremonies gave thanks for the season's hunting. At festivals throughout the Arctic, people showed off their strength and skills in sports contests. Sports included seal skinning, wrestling, dog and reindeer racing and blanket tossing.

TUG OF WAR
Two Inuit boys compete in a tug of war. This traditional sport tested the strength of both young and old. Opponents tugged on wooden handles bound by a stout strip of sealskin, as shown above. Other tests of strength included the painful sports of finger-wrestling and cheek-pulling.

SEAL SKINNING
An Inuit woman works fast to skin a seal in record time at a skinning contest held in northwest Canada. Contestants often used their teeth to grip the skin while both hands were busy with the *ulu,* or rounded skinning knife.

RACING REINDEER
A herder urges on his reindeer team during a race in Siberia. Reindeer and dog races were traditional at Arctic festivals. Hunters enjoyed the chance to show off their well-trained teams. Light sledges were used so the animals could run as fast as possible. Reindeer racing is still a popular sport in some parts of the Arctic.

SYLLABIC SYSTEM

This illustration shows the syllabic language system used by the Inuit in the Arctic. It was invented by Christian missionaries. Traditionally, Arctic languages were never written down. Each symbol represents a sound rather than a single letter. This makes it more difficult to use than alphabetic script.

LANGUAGE AND TEACHING

Inuit children work at a computer in a school in northern Canada. The words on the screen are written in syllabics. For most of the 20th century, children learned their lessons in languages such as English, Swedish and Russian. By the time they returned home, they had forgotten much of their own language and could hardly talk to their parents.

TRADITIONAL SKILLS

Two Inuit boys learn to build a sledge at school in northwest Greenland. For many years, the old skills of Arctic groups were not taught in schools. Recently, however, Arctic people have taken a new pride in their culture. Sledge-building and sewing lessons are now part of the curriculum at many schools.

HUNTING TRIP

A young Inuit boy and his father skin a reindeer they have killed on a hunting expedition. For much of the 20th century, traditional skills, such as hunting, skinning and herding, were no longer considered important. Recently, however, they have been revived. The school system has been improved, and in many schools boys are now given time off to go on hunting trips.

The Arctic Today

DURING THE SECOND HALF of the 20th century, mining continued to accelerate in the Arctic. In 1968, vast deposits of oil and gas were found at Prudhoe Bay in Alaska. Mining caused pollution and disturbed traditional ways of life. In the 1980s, there were several major disasters. The giant oil spill from the supertanker *Exxon Valdez* polluted a huge area of the Alaskan coastline, killing many plants and animals. In 1986, the Chernobyl nuclear power station in the Ukraine caught fire and released a cloud of radioactive gas. The radiation poisoned the feeding grounds of the reindeer in Lapland – a disaster for the Saami herders.

From the 1970s, Arctic groups began to organize their own response to development in the region. They laid claim to lands where their ancestors had hunted and herded for centuries. In recent years, Arctic groups have won many major land claims. In 1990, the Inuit gained a large homeland in northern Canada, which they named Nunavut. It was handed over in 1999. Today, Arctic groups take a new pride in their heritage, and lost skills are being revived.

OLD AND NEW
A Saami rides a modern snowmobile across a frozen lake in Finland. In the past, Saami herders used reindeer to pull sledges across the frozen Arctic landscape. For most Arctic people, however, life today is a mix of ancient and modern ways. The Inuit, Saami and many other Arctic groups use the new technologies of the developed world while holding onto the traditions and culture of their ancestors.

OIL MINING IN ALASKA
The Trans-Alaskan pipeline snakes for thousands of miles across the Arctic tundra, carrying oil mined at Prudhoe Bay in northern Alaska south to the ice-free port of Valdez. From there, the oil is shipped all over the world in giant supertankers. Unfortunately, the Trans-Alaskan pipeline cuts across traditional Inuit hunting grounds and caribou migration routes which have been used by the deer for thousands of years. The Trans-Alaskan pipeline is just one example of how development and industry in the Arctic has disturbed the traditional way of life in the region.

OIL SPILL

A cormorant whose feathers are clogged with oil from the *Exxon Valdez* disaster lies dead on the coast of Alaska. In 1989, the oil tanker *Exxon Valdez* struck a reef in Alaskan waters. Thousands of tonnes of oil were spilled into the sea. Alaskan coasts were polluted with the oil as it washed ashore, and thousands of sea otters, seabirds and other creatures died.

PROTEST GROUPS

Bulldozers clear the site of a new dam in 1979 whilst protesters look on in horror. Between 1979 and 1981, the Saami organized a major protest against plans to build a dam on the River Alta in Norway. Unfortunately, the protest was unsuccessful – the campaigners lost the battle to prevent construction in the courts. Peaceful protest is an essential part of a democratic society. People can get their views heard through campaigns such as these. They may even be able to influence the outcome of controversial plans.

OUR LAND

In 1999, Inuit and other Arctic groups celebrated as the large homeland of Nunavut in northern Canada was handed over to them. The name *Nunavut* means "our land" in the Inuit language. The territory is the size of Norway. Nunavut is just one of a number of land claims that have been settled in recent years. Arctic groups have also won a share in profits from mining and industrial operations conducted on their lands.

POWER OF THE PEOPLE

Young people who live in the Arctic have much to look forward to in the future. Computers and communications allow them to overcome the problems of distance and be in touch with people around the world. They can share their pride in their culture and their unique environment with visitors and also via the Internet. By the time this boy has grown up, he will be a citizen of the world, not just of the Arctic.

Glossary

A

adobe Plaster used by Pueblo Indians on their homes. It was made from clay and straw.

ajagaq An ancient spear game played by children in the Arctic.

Algonquian A group of many tribes (including the Secotan and Powhatan) who shared the northeast coastal areas.

amaut A back pouch used to carry Inuit babies and young children.

angakok A name for an Inuit shaman (medicine man).

anorak An Inuit word meaning an outer jacket.

archaeologist A person who studies ancient remains or ruins.

Arctic Region in the far north of our planet, around the North Pole.

Arctic Circle An imaginary line circling the Earth at a latitude of 66° 33' North that marks the limit of the Arctic. All areas inside the Arctic Circle experience at least one day a year when the sun never sets, and one day when it never rises.

B

baleen The horny plates which hang down inside the mouths of some whales and which are used to filter small sea creatures, the whale's food, from the water.

bark The outer layer (covering) of tree trunks.

beluga A small, white-skinned Arctic whale.

blizzard A strong wind that blows at the same time as a heavy snowfall.

blubber A layer of fat found under the skin of seals, whales and walruses, which helps them keep warm in icy water.

bow drill An ancient tool used to start a fire by creating heat.

C

cache To hide a store of food, or the food store itself.

caribou Reindeer found in North America.

cavalry Soldiers on horseback.

Chukchi A reindeer-herding people of northeastern Siberia.

clan A group of people who are related to each other.

Cold War A time of hostility between the West and the Soviet Union. It followed World War II and lasted until the 1980s.

colonies Communities or groups of people who settle in another land, but still keep links with their own country.

congress Assembly of people who govern the separate states.

continent Name for the large areas of land that cover the Earth. The continents are Antarctica, North and South America, Asia, Africa, Australia and Europe.

cradleboard A wooden board, usually with protective head area, to which a baby was strapped and carried about.

currency A form of exchange for goods such as money or wampum.

D

descendant A person who is descended from (born after) an individual or group of people who lived earlier.

dialects Regional accents and language variations.

Distance Early Warning (DEW) A line of radar stations that were built across the American Arctic.

drag handle A tool that is used to haul animal carcasses across the ice and snow.

dugout canoe A canoe made by hollowing out a tree trunk.

E

effigy A figure or doll representing someone.

Evenk A once-nomadic people of eastern Siberia.

F

federal The central government of a federation (a group).

fiord A narrow coastal inlet found in Scandinavia, where the land falls steeply to the sea.

floe A floating sheet of sea-ice.

frontiers Land on the border between Indian territory and land European settlers had already taken or bought.

G

glyphs Pictures that tell a message or have a meaning.

H

harpoon A spear-like weapon attached to a long line that is used to catch whales and seals.

hunter-gatherer A person who lives by hunting animals and gathering wild roots and other plants.

I

Ice Age One of a number of times in the Earth's history when large parts of the planet surface became covered with ice.

iceberg An enormous chunk of ice that floats in the sea.

ice cap A mass of ice that permanently covers land in the polar regions. Greenland has the largest ice cap in the Arctic.

ice floes Large sheets of ice floating in the sea.

igloo An Inuit word meaning house, often used to refer to Inuit shelters built of ice blocks.

immigrants People who come to live in a land from other countries.

inua An Inuit word that means spirit.

Inuit The native people of the North American Arctic, Canada and Greenland as distinguished from Asia and the Aleutian islands. Inuit is also the general name for an Eskimo in Canada.

inuksuk A stone column made by Inuit hunters, used to herd caribou into an ambush.

Iroquois A group of tribes from the Woodlands who joined together to form a powerful government.

ivory The hard, smooth, cream-coloured part of the tusks of elephants and walruses.

J

joik Traditional Saami improvised songs that tell the story of the day's events.

K

kakivak A three-pronged Inuit spear used to catch fish.

kamik Sealskin boots.

kayak A one-person Inuit canoe powered by a double-bladed paddle.

kiva An underground chamber used for religious ceremonies among Pueblo people.

Kwatee A mythical figure connected with tales of the creation of the universe.

L

lacrosse A stick and ball game played with a stick with a net on the end.

land bridge An area of dry land joining two land masses. In prehistoric times, a land bridge linked the continents of Asia and North America.

Lapp *see* Saami

latitude Imaginary lines that run parallel to the Equator of the Earth, going north and south. The Equator, running round the centre of the Earth, is 0°. The North Pole is 90°N and the South Pole is 90°S. Latitude is used by geographers to calculate the positions of places.

legend An ancient story that has been handed down over the years. It may be part myth and part truth.

legislation Making laws.

lichen A living organism that grows on rocks in the Arctic and is eaten by caribou.

loom A frame used for weaving yarn into fabric and blankets.

M

mammal A type of warm-blooded animal such as human beings, whales, cats, and bats.

migration A seasonal journey made by people or animals to find food or avoid extreme cold.

missionary Someone sent by a religious organization to a country to do religious and social work.

moccasins Soft leather, slip-on shoes often decorated with beads.

mukluk Deerskin boots.

muktuk A gristly layer found just below a whale's skin, eaten as a delicacy in the Arctic.

myth An old tale or legend that describes gods, spirits or fantastic creatures.

N

narwhal A species of small Arctic whale.

nation A group of people who live in one territory and usually share the same language or history.

Nenet A reindeer-herding people of western Siberia.

nomads People who move from one area to another to find food, better land or to follow herds.

North Pole The most northerly point on the Earth.

Nunavut A large Inuit territory in northern Canada, established 1999.

O

obsidian A dark, glassy volcanic rock found in the earth.

Oglala Sioux A band of the Western or Teton Sioux.

P

pack ice Floating sea-ice.

parka A hooded, warm overcoat usually made of caribou or other animal skin and worn by Inuit people in the Arctic.

pelts The skin or fur of a furry animal such as a beaver.

pemmican Food mixture made from minced bison meat, berries and animal fat.

permafrost Permanently frozen ground. Permafrost can reach depths of 600m in some areas.

peske A thick fur parka worn by Saami people over their tunics.

pictographs Picture writing.

plankton Tiny plants and animals that drift on a sea or lake.

prospector A person who searches for valuable minerals such as gold.

Pueblo People from the Southwest who lived in villages built of mud and stone.

pulkka A boat-shaped sleigh used in Siberia and Scandinavia.

Q

quahog An edible round clam found in North America.

R

reservation An area of land chosen by the United States government and set aside for a tribe(s) in the 1800s. Sometimes early reservation land was seized again later by the US and tribes were moved on again to another reservation further away.

rite A solemn procedure normally carried out for a religious purpose or part of a ceremony.

ritual An often repeated set of actions carried out during a religious or other ceremony.

S

Saami The ancient people of Lapland in Scandinavia.

sauna A bath of hot steam.

scalps Chunks of skin and long hair that warriors shaved off the heads of their enemies in battle.

settlers People who came from other countries to settle or stay in North America.

shaman The medicine man or woman of the tribe. These people were spiritual and ceremonial leaders and doctors.

shrine A holy place used for worship, often built beside graves.

sinew The tissue that connects an animal's bones and muscles.

slingshot Another name for a catapult.

Stallos People-eating monsters in Saami legends.

sweat lodge An earth-covered lodge or structure built from saplings and covered with blankets, canvas or hide in which a steam bath was taken.

T

taboo A rule or custom linked with religious beliefs that shows respect to the spirits.

taiga A belt of forests found in the far north, south of the tundra.

tipi A conical tent with a frame of poles, covered with animal skins, used by Plains Indians.

toboggan A wooden frame on runners used for sliding over snow and ice.

tomahawk A war axe. Its head was of stone, metal or bone.

totem A good luck charm.

totem pole A tall post carved with totems.

trading post A general store where people from a wide area traded or swapped goods.

tradition The habits, beliefs or practices handed down from one generation to the next.

trappers People who trap animals, especially for their fur and skin.

travois A V-shaped frame for carrying possessions dragged by dogs and later by horses.

treaty A peace agreement.

tribe A group of people who shared a common language and way of life.

tundra The barren, treeless lowlands of the far north.

U

ulu A rounded knife used mostly by Inuit women to skin and cut meat.

umiak An open boat, powered by oars and sometimes sails, used by the Inuit to hunt whales.

W

wampum Shells, or beads made from shells, strung together and used as currency or to record a historical event.

whalebone *see* baleen

wigwam A dwelling made of bark, rushes or skins spread over arched poles lashed together.

wolverine A furry mammal that looks like a small bear, found in many of the northern forests of Europe, Asia and North America.

Y

yagushka Traditional jacket worn by Nenet women.

Yakut A reindeer-herding people of northern Siberia.

Index

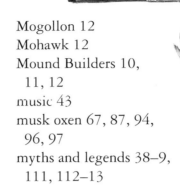